from
noodles
to
strudels

volume two

BY LILY ROSMAN AND RUTH LASMAN

from noodles to strudels

volume two

ART BY LEONA HERTZBERG AND JOE JOYCE

Henrietta Szold
120th ANNIVERSARY

HADASSAH, the Women's Zionist Organization of American, Inc.
Proceeds to support its programs in Israel and the U.S.A.

FROM NOODLES TO STRUDELS, VOLUME TWO is published by the women of the Beverly Hills Chapter of HADASSAH, the Women's Zionist Organization of America. This is the 120th anniversary year of the birth of Miss Henrietta Szold, American-Jewish scholar, writer and pioneer Zionist. Founded by Miss Szold in 1912, HADASSAH now numbers over 370,000 members. HADASSAH is the Hebrew name of courageous Queen Esther in the Biblical story of Purim. It is also the Hebrew equivalent of the "myrtle", a plant indigenous to the soil of Israel, symbolizing everlasting life.

HADASSAH originated as a study group. Its education programs have a two-fold thrust — the understanding of our Jewish heritage of ethical and moral values as well as the American struggle for freedom and equality. Study leads to action. In their local communities HADASSAH women are involved in tutorial, nutritional, medical screening and refugee settlement programs. Through HADASSAH's youth movement Hashachar (The Dawn), they ensure that committed young people of today become dedicated leaders of tomorrow.

The impact of HADASSAH on contemporary Israel is felt in every corner of the land. HADASSAH's broad program of medicine, medical teaching and research, vocational education, child rescue and rehabilitation and land reclamation affects the lives of all Israeli citizens. Through the Jewish National Fund HADASSAH has participated in the reclamation of tens of thousands of acres for farming and industrial sites. Over 1000 students are enrolled yearly in HADASSAH's Comprehensive High School and 2-year Community College providing Israel with vitally needed technical and para-professional personnel. HADASSAH is the major contributor to Youth Aliyah, the youth immigration movement which has rescued and settled over 175,000 Jewish children in Israel. Founded in 1934 to snatch thousands from the furnaces of the holocaust in Germany, Youth Aliyah currently cares for 19,000 young people annually.

The Hadassah-Hebrew University Medical Center, Ein Karem and the Hadassah University Hospital, Mt. Scopus, Jerusalem are the cornerstone of HADASSAH's medical program in Israel. Both facilities, with 1100 beds, service an annual inpatient load of 33,000. There are 4,000 medical personnel and 500 volunteers. Outpatient visits are 400,000 yearly. Millions of dollars are spent annually in the United States for equipment. To date nearly 5,000 students have graduated from the schools of Medicine, Dentistry, Pharmacy, Nursing, Public Health and Occupational Therapy. HADASSAH research projects merit grants from governments, institutes and foundations all over the world. Over 1,000 research papers are published annually.

HADASSAH's motto is Jeremiah's ancient message "the healing of the daughter of my people". It is the promise of life and hope to countless sufferers, Jewish, Moslem and Christian who benefit from HADASSAH's programs of healing, teaching and research.

Proceeds from the sale of FROM NOODLES TO STRUDELS, VOLUME TWO will go to maintain all the above projects.

25,000 volumes and 8 years later, we are proud to present "Noodles to Strudels, Volume Two." Since the phenomenal success of the culinary potpourri, Beverly Hills Hadassah called "From Noodles to Strudels" we have received many recipes from members who wanted to participate in another book. Going through the shoe box filled with chocolate stained scraps of paper, backs of envelopes and neatly typed cards "from the kitchens of —," we realized we had enough mouthwatering material for Volume Two.

We assembled a group of well traveled, creative cooks who shared their precious recipes, prepared, tasted and criticized for eight months. We all came from a variety of cooking traditions and our discussions were heated, earnest and objective. A consensus had to be reached on every recipe so that even a novice could try a recipe for company and be confident of success. Joe Joyce, who created the eye-catching cover and designed Volume One, generously worked with us again. The enchanting drawings by Leona Hertzberg, which charmed everyone in our first book, add to the continuity and attractiveness of Volume Two. Penny Zachary, our resident author, raconteur and wit helped us with the sparkling captions.

The past decade has revealed surprisingly many changes. Most Beverly Hills Hadassah kitchens have food processors. Chores that were too time consuming for busy volunteers can now be done in seconds by a machine. We have added the wok to our arsenal to fight skyrocketing prices of food. We've discovered how far a chicken and a little beef with stretch, blended with the exotic spices of the East. We have become health conscious, cutting down on sugars, salt and eggs and reading labels carefully. But our desserts are delectable and most of them are not life threatening. Though we have borrowed something from cuisines of many lands, our favorites are our Jewish recipes. These treasures are a link in the chain of our own heritage from mother to daughter and will always identify a Jewish table and the Baleboosteh* who manages a Jewish home.

The hours devoted to this project have been a labor of love. We are grateful for the priceless gift of friendship and cameraderie of all who worked with us. We thank Esther Cooper, Dorothy Gelman and Claire Gordon who did the preliminary typing; Joan Kheel, Shirley Kirsch and Joyce Leytus who helped proofread; our Chapter Presidents, Shirley Kirsch and Ossie Walman who encouraged us all the way. We applaud everyone connected with Volume One. They blazed the trail and we followed in their creative footsteps. Together with all our readers we will have the satisfaction of contributing to the support of the projects of HADASSAH.

Create with feeling, measure with care and serve with love.
Ruth Lasman and Lily Rosman, Editors

*Yiddish for an excellent and praiseworthy homemaker.

RUTH LASMAN is a native of Sioux City, Iowa and her parents came from Roumania. She has remembered and wrenched old secret recipes from friends and family all over the country. She was the Beverly Hills Hadassah president under whose administration Volume One was begun. With her co-editor she has reviewed, rewritten and retyped every recipe. In addition, her expertise in the printing field has ensured that the high standard set by our first book has been maintained.

LILY ROSMAN is a past president of the Beverly Hills Chapter of Hadassah. She was born in Italy, her parents came from Germany, her in-laws from Russia and Poland. Lily gathered together and inspired the testing committee, cooked, typed and coordinated the many details of producing this book in her own well-organized way. Although she is busy with many community activities, she enjoys entertaining her family and friends.

the testing committee

All the members of our testing committee have been active in Beverly Hills Hadassah for many years. For this project they met every week for 8 months in each other's homes, testing all the recipes that were received and contributing many treasured ones of their own. Their good taste and skill are evident.

DODIE BIENENFELD was born in Chicago. She is a splendid cook who has been an avid pupil of both her mother and mother-in-law. Her mother was a celebrated gourmet cook. Her mother-in-law is justifiably famous for her delicious traditional Jewish dishes. Dodie's Rosh Hashana dessert table is a beautiful visual tableau and a feast of flavors. You will find many of this talented family's recipes in our book.

DEENA BIREN was our mentor for the Chinese recipes. After a guided tour of the specialty markets in Chinatown, she directed us step by step in her demonstration kitchen and generously shared recipes from her classes. Deena was one of the first of our crowd to have the daring and skill to prepare complete Chinese banquets at home. Her classes in Chinese cooking have been eagerly attended and have contributed to the explosion of interest in Chinese cooking in our community. She has recently traveled to China.

BEATRICE BOISH is a former New Yorker and a graduate of the New York Institute of Dietetics. She has successfully catered many charitable luncheons and teas. She was a Lawry's cook off participant and received a trophy for the Geoff Edwards KMPC favorite recipe award. Bea is the co-author of our popular "From Noodles to Strudels". She tested and developed many new recipes for this book.

JOAN BRAM's country kitchen reflects her warm hospitality and love of cooking. All eight burners on her restaurant size stove are constantly busy. Her wok is definitely seasoned. Pots and pans of all shapes and sizes hang from the ceiling. She is always trying new recipes from many countries and finds any excuse to prepare a petit lunch or grand buffet.

LORE GROSS was born in Germany. Her small intimate dinner parties are a delight to the eye and palate. She has generously shared many of her flavorful old world recipes which blend elegance with tradition.

MIMI GROSSMAN hails from Texas. She brought another accent and another region to our committee. As a tester for "Bon Appetit" Magazine she brought a professional dimension to our sessions. Mimi's cooking classes are also very popular.

RUTH LOW is a second generation Israeli. Guests from many countries are entertained in her home and share recipes from their native lands and embassies. She has traveled all over the world, but we especially enjoyed the flavor of Israel that she added to our book.

CLAIRE SCHWEITZER is a native of Pennsylvania. She is a virtuoso cook whose skills are praised by family and many friends lucky enough to have dined at her table. She has inherited a meticulous attention to detail from her mother, a true "Yiddishe Mama," whose talented hands demonstrated our delicious knishes; and she is passing her appreciation and understanding of gourmet cooking to her four sons, one of whom is a fledgling chef of distinction.

JUDY WILKIN's family is from England, so her culinary heritage is high tea and trifle. Busy as a P.T.A. president, Hadassah executive and mother of four young children she still finds time to teach microwave cooking to other young women who want to cook lavishly but don't have the time to spend hours in the kitchen.

JUDY ZEIDLER's name is a household word in this community where her column and recipes on Jewish holiday cooking appears regularly in the prestigious Los Angeles Times. She and her husband belong to numerous wine and food societies. She teaches kosher Jewish cooking and lately has developed classes devoted entirely to chocolate and the newest "rage," homemade pasta. Her bubbly personality and down-to-earth approach inspired all of us to try new combinations of flavors and techniques.

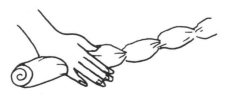

cherished recipes
shared by women who care

Sydelle Acheatel
Shelly Adler
Nancy Barth
Ina Barth
Sarah Bauman
Leslie Benbassat
Eunice Berman
Ann Berenson
Dodie Bienenfeld
Esther Bienenfeld
Muriel Bienenfeld
Manya Bindman
Deena Biren
Mitzi Blahd
Georgie Block
Natalie Block
Sarah Blum
Shirley Blumenthal
Marlene Blumert
Beatrice Boish
Joan Bram
Ethel Brodie
Toby Brooks
Millie Cramer
Sunnie Cramer
Bea David
June Deckman
Mary Dubrow
Gertrude Evans
Bernice Feldheim
Cathy Feldman
Frieda Felsher
Lisa J. Feldman
Beverly Firestein
Tamar Freeman
Tula Friedman
Sylvia Frischling
Sybil Frischling
Kaoru Fukuhara
Magda Garcia

Betty Gardner
Sonya Gelfand
Cinda Lee Gelman
Dorothy Gellman
Grace Gries
Selma Goldberg
Ann Goldenberg
Fran Goodfield
Claire Gordon
Ruth Gottesman
Dorothy Gould
Lore Gross
Mimi Grossman
Esther Harris
Ruth Helfman
Mildred Hirson
Laurie Hoover
Sara Horowitz
Libby Isaac
Myrtle Karp
Joan Kheel
Rose Kilgorn
Louise Kornberg
Helen Klein
Jane Kramer
Mimi Landres
Ellien Landy
Marian Lasman
Ruth Lasman
Juanita Lee
Sadie Lee
Jennifer Levinson
Syde Levinthal
Helen Levin
Susan Levich
Sarah Lewis
Selma Lewis
Cecille Lieberthal
Doris E. Lounsbury
Ruth Low

10

Ethel Lozabnick
Maxine Meyers
Bess Millet
Gladys Mogerman
Carole Oken
Cecille Priver
Esther Priver
Kitty Pasternak
Marilyn Rosen
Betty Rosenwasser
Lily Rosman
Beverly Robbins
Ilene Samson
Diane Sands
Hemda Sassoon
Barbara Schecter
Florence Schneider
Barbara Schwartz
Edythe Schwartz
Claire Schweitzer

Dee Sheinbein
Betty Shepard
Thanya Shulkin
Esther Siegel
Evelyn Sidney
Helen Simon
Sharon Simon
Frances Stawisky
Ruth Swerdlow
Rose Tabah
Estelle Tuchler
Joan Vigdoff
Ossie Walman
Libby Wertheim
Harriet White
Clara Widiss
Judy Wilkin
Annetta Winnick
Shirlee Yarbrow
Judy Zeidler

general instructions

All recipes in this book are appropriate for kosher kitchens. Dairy products (cream, sour cream, butter) may always be substituted for their non-dairy equivalents; however, the resulting dish may no longer be acceptable under the Jewish dietary laws.

Butter and margarine used in these recipes are always unsalted. All margarines are the non-dairy variety.

The flour used is always "all purpose" unless otherwise stated.

Herbs are dried unless otherwise stated.

All measurements are level.

The temperatures given are for pre-heated ovens.

Read the entire recipe through from beginning to end before you start cooking.

3 tsp	=	1 TB
16 TB	=	1 C
5 TB + 1 tsp	=	1/3 C
2 TB oil	=	1 oz
1 stick butter	=	¼ lb or ½ C
1 lb butter or solid shortening	=	2 C

contents

hadassah hints

An easy way to reduce your electric bill is to eliminate the drying cycle on the dishwasher. Upon completion of the rinse cycle, turn the dial to "off" and open door to let steam escape and dishes air dry.

When making a large number of meat balls, roll and place them on a shallow cookie sheet. To brown, place tray in oven at 350 degrees for 30 minutes, turning often. Drain fat off and freeze on cookie sheet. Store the frozen meat balls in plastic bags. Use as needed.

The best oil for seasoning cutting boards and salad bowls is mineral oil. It is tasteless, odorless and does not turn rancid.

To help whipped cream retain texture when not served immediately, add 1 tsp light corn syrup to each half pint of cream before whipping.

Egg whites achieve fuller volume when beaten at room temperature.

If you are watching your salt intake, use the powdered form when buying spices, e.g. garlic powder instead of garlic salt.

SEASONED SALT
½ C salt
½ tsp garlic powder
½ tsp thyme
½ tsp marjoram
3 tsp paprika
½ tsp turmeric
½ tsp onion powder
¼ tsp dill weed

FINE HERBS
2 tsp dried basil
2 tsp dried marjoram
2 tsp dried oregano
2 tsp dried rosemary
2 tsp dried thyme
1 tsp sage

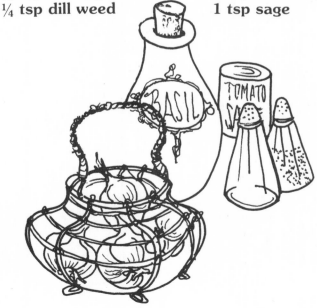

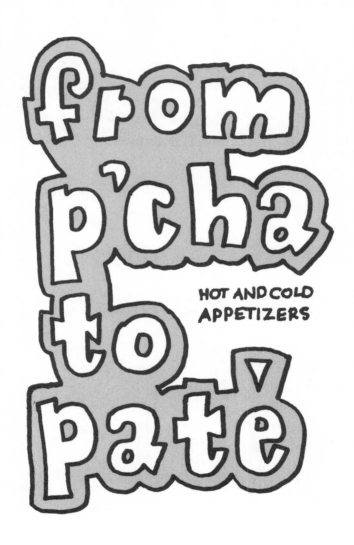

from p'cha to paté

HOT AND COLD APPETIZERS

sunburst artichoke

Start with something pretty

1 large artichoke, cooked and cooled*
3 oz cream cheese
1 oz blue cheese
½ tsp garlic powder
½ tsp Worcestershire sauce
¼ cup finely chopped walnuts, toasted
1 small can black olives, pitted and drained
1 tsp olive oil

Have cheeses at room temperature. Mash together and add garlic powder and Worcestershire sauce. Blend well.

Peel the artichoke. Spread a small amount of cheese mixture over edible part of each leaf. Sprinkle with chopped nuts.

Place olives in a bowl. Add 1 tsp of olive oil to coat. Slice each olive in half. Place on each leaf, cut side down. Arrange leaves in a circle on a large round platter. Garnish with a flower in the center.

*When you cook artichokes, add 1 TB fresh lemon juice to the boiling water to keep the leaves green.

strudel by "the book"

Made with filo leaves
Use your favorite filling

Lightly dampen a dish towel. Cover it with wax paper. Unfold the filo leaves and place on top of the paper. Fold the leaves, wax paper and towel over in half like a book. The towel becomes the "book cover". Open the book to the "first page" and brush with melted butter. Sprinkle lightly with bread crumbs or ground almonds (optional). Repeat on each page until you get to the center. Do not butter center. Close the book.

Starting from the back, repeat process going towards the center. With the book open at the center, spread your filling on the lower third of the page. Fold in the ends at the left and right. Roll the strudel as a jelly roll using the towel and wax paper to help you. Place seam side down on an ungreased baking sheet. Brush top with melted butter. Strudel may be prepared ahead to this point.

If you refrigerate it, bring it back to room temperature before baking. If you freeze it, allow butter to freeze, then cover. Defrost 30 minutes before baking, and bake a few minutes longer. Bake 12 minutes in a 350 degree oven. Remove from the oven. Brush with more melted butter. Score diagonally to make 1½ inch pieces. Return to the oven and bake 15 more minutes.

Use 10 leaves at a time. Use about ¼ lb melted unsalted butter for each 10 leaves.

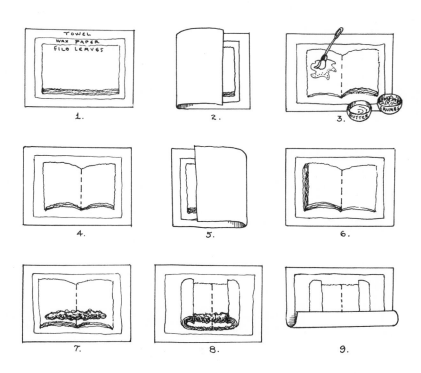

cabbage strudel

Be prepared to take a bow

1 lb package filo dough
1 lb butter, melted
2 C bread crumbs

FILLING:
2 TB butter
2 TB oil
4 TB flour
3 C chopped onions
4 medium heads cabbage, shredded
2 TB paprika
1/3 C brown sugar
salt and pepper to taste

Melt butter and oil together until bubbly. Add flour, cooking slowly and stirring until brown. Add onions, cook slowly, stirring about 10 minutes. Add cabbage, sugar, paprika, salt and pepper and cook an additional 45 minutes. Cool.

Work with 4-5 sheets of filo at one time, keeping the rest covered with a damp towel. Place 4 sheets, one on top of the other. Fold in half and close like a book. Open first page. Brush with melted butter and sprinkle with crumbs. Turn "pages" and repeat brushing with butter and crumbs until you get to center. Don't brush center with butter. Close "book" and open again from the back, brushing each page with butter and sprinkling with crumbs. When you get to the center, brush with butter and sprinkle with crumbs. Spread ¼ of the filling across bottom. Fold ends over and roll into a "jellyroll". Spread with melted butter. Repeat procedure, to make 4 rolls.

Refrigerate, until butter hardens. May be frozen at this point. Brush with beaten egg (optional). Score at 2″ intervals through first layer of dough, so that steam will escape. Bake at 350 degrees for 45 minutes. Slice immediately. Serve hot with sour cream and fresh dill.

mellow grapefruit

2 grapefruit, cut in half and sectioned
2 TB melted butter or margarine
½ C brown sugar
4 maraschino cherries
¼ C apricot brandy

Pour melted butter over grapefruit halves. Sprinkle brown sugar over each grapefruit half and place a cherry in the center. Pour 2 TB brandy over grapefruit. Broil for about 3 minutes. Add the rest of the brandy just before serving.

smoked salmon spread

Lovely to look at and easy to make

1 lb smoked salmon (lox) bits
¼ C lemon juice
½ lb unsalted butter
1 C sour cream
salt and pepper to taste
Garnishes: lemon slices, capers, snipped fresh dill

Puree salmon and lemon juice in blender or processor. Melt butter. Add to salmon mixture in slow steady stream while blending. Remove to a bowl. Fold in sour cream, salt and pepper. Place in a 2½ C mold and chill. Unmold, garnish and serve with Melba toast or crackers. Serves 40-50 as an appetizer.

herring melange

A travelling hors d'oeuvre for boats, picnics or the Hollywood Bowl
Must be prepared 3 days ahead

1 jar wine herring snacks (12 oz) drained and diced
6 oz marinated artichoke hearts, drained and diced
6 oz pitted black olives, drained and sliced
1 green pepper, diced
1 red onion, diced
12 oz chili sauce

Mix all together, chop by hand or in processor, depending on the texture you like. Refrigerate at least 3 days. Serve on rye bread or with crackers. Lasts 3 weeks in refrigerator. Serves 15-20 as an appetizer.

broiled curry appetizer

Not to worry curry

1 pkg English muffins (6) split and toasted
1 C chopped black olives
½ C chopped green onions
1½ C shredded cheddar or longhorn cheese
½ C mayonnaise
1 tsp mild curry powder
salt to taste if desired

Combine all ingredients and spoon onto muffin halves. Broil until cheese melts. Cut into quarter wedges and serve hot. Makes 48.

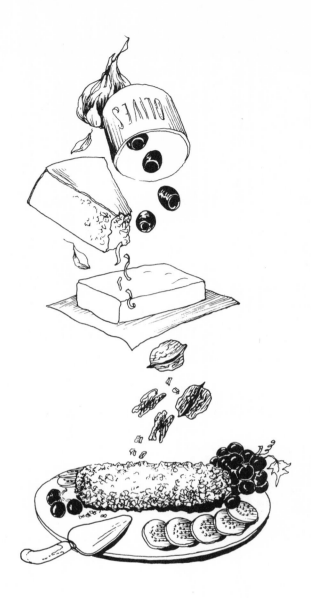

cheese ball

8 oz cream cheese
8 oz cheddar cheese, grated
3 oz chive cheese
1 small can olives, drained and chopped
3 cloves garlic, crushed
1 C chopped nuts (walnuts)

Soften cream cheese and mix well with other softened cheeses and olives and garlic. Shape into a ball. Roll into chopped nuts. Wrap in foil. Chill 24 hours. Serve at room temperature with crackers. May be frozen and thawed to room temperature on day of serving.

cheese bourrekas

FILLING
8 oz cream cheese
½ lb feta cheese
1 egg
½ tsp salt

DOUGH
1 heaping tsp baking powder
4 C flour
½ lb margarine, unsalted
1 C milk
1 egg yolk, beaten
sesame seeds

Combine the two cheeses, salt and egg. Let stand. Add baking powder to the flour and cut in the margarine until flour looks like meal. Using 1/3 of the milk, combine 1/3 of the flour mix and knead lightly into a ball. Roll out into a small sheet. Cut into 3 inch rounds and fill with a heaping tsp of the cheese mixture. Continue to roll small sheets of dough until used up.* Fold rounds in half and pinch together in a ruffled pattern.

Brush with a beaten egg yolk and sprinkle with sesame seeds. Bake in 350 degree oven for 20 minutes or until the bourrekas are light golden in color. Makes 60.

*When you add small amounts of milk to the flour, the dough is not sticky.

cheese and fruit log

An interesting combination of flavors

8 oz cream cheese, at room temperature
¼ C white wine
¼ tsp salt
1 lb sharp cheddar cheese, shredded
1 tsp caraway seeds
½ C dried apricots, finely chopped

Beat cream cheese and wine with salt until fluffy. Blend in other ingredients. Refrigerate ½ hour. Turn out on a sheet of foil and shape into a roll. Wrap in foil and chill at least 2 hours, or overnight. Serve with pumpernickel or crackers.

marinated japanese eggplant

    1 lb small Japanese eggplants
    3 oz olive oil
    1 oz vinegar
    4 cloves garlic
    salt and pepper to taste

Wash eggplants. Cut stems and cut lengthwise into quarters if very small or into 6 parts each. In a small stainless steel or enamel pot mix oil, vinegar, salt and pepper to taste. Peel and slice garlic cloves very thin. Add to oil mixture.

Keep heat on low, add eggplant slices and simmer for about 8 minutes. Cool and store in a covered glass dish. Serve cold in its own juice.

gravlax with akvavit

Epicurean elegance

    2-3 lb salmon fillet (fresh)
    ¼ C coarse salt
    1 tsp ground white pepper
    2 TB sugar
    1 bunch fresh dill or 1 tsp dry dill
    ½ C Akvavit (the Danish national drink)

Combine seasonings and rub on both sides of fish. Place in a glass dish. Sprinkle with ½ C Akvavit. Cover with wax paper and weigh down. Chill for three days basting and turning every 12 hours. Brush excess dill and sauce off. Slice thinly.Serve with mustard dill sauce, or a selection of chopped onion, egg, capers or cream cheese and thinly sliced dark rye bread.

mustard dill sauce

    2 TB white wine vinegar
    2 TB sugar
    2 tsp dry mustard
    1/3 C minced fresh or 1 tsp dry dill
    1 tsp Bavarian mustard
    pepper to taste
    1/3 C vegetable oil

Blend throughly, mixing oil with a whisk one tablespoon at a time. Chill.

eggplant appetizer
"PUTLAJEL"
An authentic Roumanian recipe

1 medium eggplant
1 small onion, chopped fine
½ C salad oil
salt, pepper

Broil the eggplant in the oven for about 10 minutes on each side, or until it is soft all over when pierced with a toothpick. When it is cool enough to handle, cut in two and carefully scoop out the pulp into a chopping bowl.

Add the onion, salad oil, salt, pepper and chop thoroughly. Chill and serve. Garnish with slices of tomatoes.

ISRAELI VERSION: Add 4 hard cooked eggs. Chop with the eggplant mixture.

ANOTHER COUNTRY HEARD FROM:
1 medium size eggplant
2 ripe tomatoes, peeled
2 stalks celery, diced
½ large green pepper
2 large eggs, hard boiled
juice of 1 lemon
2 TB salad oil, more if necessary
½ tsp salt
1 tsp sugar, or to taste

Bake eggplant on an oiled pie pan in the oven at 350 degrees until eggplant tests tender when pierced with a fork. When cool, peel and scoop out the meat to a wooden chopping bowl. Add the tomatoes, celery, green pepper, eggs, lemon juice, oil, salt and sugar. Chop finely. Chill until flavors blend. Serve on lettuce leaf. Garnish with black olives, slices of tomato or green onion.

tuna dip italiano
You'd never know it's tuna

1 envelope Italian salad dressing mix
1½ C sour cream
1-2 tsp lemon juice
6½ oz canned tuna, drained and flaked
1 egg, hard boiled, chopped

Place all ingredients in a bowl and blend throughly. Makes 2 cups. Serve with raw vegetables or crackers.

filo triangles

Flaky tidbits — the fillings are endless

Fresh filo leaves handle easier. If you use frozen leaves follow directions on package to defrost all filo leaves evenly. One 1 lb package contains about 20 leaves. Each leaf can be cut into 4 strips, making 80 2" x 2" x 3" triangles. You will need about 1½ lbs filling and ¼ lb melted butter or margarine for 80 triangles.

Unfold the filo leaves. Place them on wax paper. Cover completely with wax paper and a damp towel to prevent them from drying out. Work with one leaf at a time, keeping the rest covered. Brush sheet with melted butter. Cut sheet into 4 strips. Place filling in corner of strip. Fold into triangle. Brush with melted butter. Sprinkle with sesame seeds (optional).

Refrigerate to harden butter before baking. Bake on greased baking sheet at 375 degrees 10-15 minutes until golden, turning once. If frozen, defrost about 30 minutes before baking. Freeze very well.

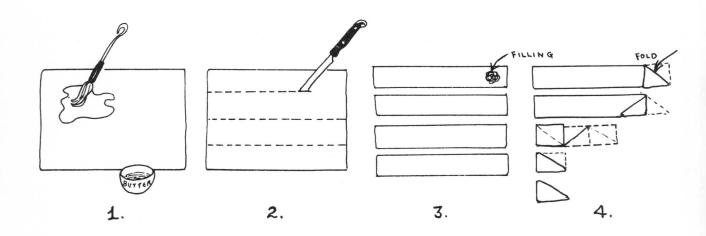

1.   2.   3.   4.

MUSHROOM FILLING
4 TB margarine
¼ C chopped onions
1 lb mushrooms, finely minced
1 TB fresh chopped parsley
½ tsp dried basil
½ tsp salt
2 TB Madeira wine

Saute onions in margarine until soft. Add mushrooms and seasonings and herbs and wine. Cook until mushrooms are soft and liquid has cooked down. Fills 20 triangles.

filo triangle fillings

SPINACH CHEESE
1 10 oz pkg frozen spinach, thawed, cooked, well drained
¼ C chopped green onions, sauteed until soft in 1 TB butter
½ lb feta cheese, crumbled
2 beaten eggs
½ C milk
2 TB chopped fresh parsley
salt and pepper to taste

ARTICHOKE HEARTS
1 pkg frozen artichoke hearts, cooked according to
    directions on package
2 TB minced scallions sauteed in oil
¼ lb ricotta cheese
½ C gruyere cheese, shredded
1/3 C parmesan cheese, grated
¼ C sour cream
2 beaten eggs
¼ tsp crushed tarragon
salt and pepper to taste

CHEESE MEDLEY
½ lb cream cheese
¼ C crumbled feta cheese
½ C grated gruyere
3 TB minced fresh parsley
1 beaten egg
salt and pepper to taste

Cheeses should be at room temperature. Blend all together. Fills 40 triangles, using 10 filo sheets.

karate knishes

We watched Manya demonstrate these with her nimble fingers

        3 C flour
        ¾ C lukewarm water
        2 eggs
        3 TB oil
        ½ tsp salt

Make well in the flour. Pour water and oil in the center, mixing all ingredients together quickly to avoid lumps, using wooden spoon or paddle. Beat until dough has elastic consistency. Roll in a bit of flour on a board to form a soft ball.

Knead with quick motion with palm of hand, adding a bit of flour as needed. Knead for about 10 minutes. Put ½ tsp of oil in a bowl. Roll your finished ball into it. Cover with clean cloth. Let it sit for 20 minutes.

CHEESE FILLING
2½ lbs hoop cheese, at room temperature
1 lb cream cheese, softened
6 eggs
½ C sugar
½ tsp salt

Mix all together. Begin rolling dough out on large board. Then cover table 36″ x 48″ with large clean cloth. Lightly flour the cloth. Using a long rolling pin, roll out dough into a large oval that covers almost the whole table. Brush with oil.

Spoon cheese filling all around the edge, leaving a space at opposite ends. Roll towards the center into 2 long rolls, carefully stretching dough as you roll. Cut along the middle. With side of hand, with motion like a karate chop, cut dough every 2″. Separate and turn each knish on its side and pinch to form a "belly button". Place on oiled pan. Brush with oil. Bake at 350 degrees for 30 minutes.

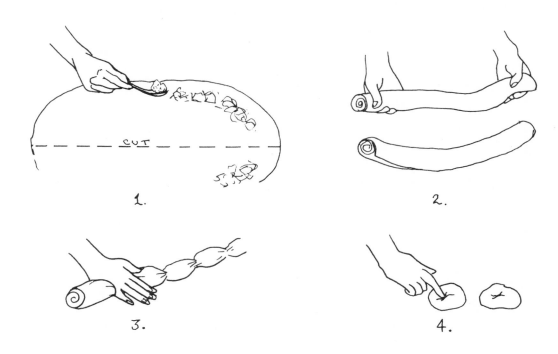

1.   2.

3.   4.

POTATO KNISHES

FILLING
4 lb potatoes, mashed
3 onions, finely chopped, sauteed in 3 TB oil
3 eggs, beaten

Another way of handling the dough: cut dough in 4″ circles. Put 1 TB filling in each circle. Gather dough up in the middle and press down.

LIVER AND MUSHROOM KNISHES

FILLING
½ lb mushrooms
1 lb chicken livers
2 large onions
salt and pepper to taste
1 clove garlic mashed

Saute livers and mushrooms and onions in 2 TB oil. Chop all together.

OR USE FROZEN PUFF PASTRY — THE EASY WAY

Defrost one sheet as directed on package. Cut sheet into thirds where it is scored. On lightly floured board, roll each until double the width. Put filling along edge lengthwise. Roll into long rolls. Seal with a little water.

Cut each roll into 5-7 knishes. Turn on side. Push down. Seal with beaten egg. Bake at 350 degrees for 30 minutes. Makes 21 small or 15 large knishes.

FILLING
½ lb hoop cheese
2 beaten eggs (reserve 3 TB for glaze)
4 oz cream cheese
2 TB sugar
pinch of salt

mini pizzas
With maxi flavor

8 oz sharp cheddar cheese, grated
8 oz can tomato sauce
4½ oz chopped olives, black
¼ tsp garlic salt
⅛ tsp oregano
2 TB oil (optional)
1 pound twin sour dough french bread (8 oz small loaves)

Mix cheese, tomato sauce, olives, spices and oil together. Let stand for several hours or overnight. Cut bread into ¼ inch slices. Spread cheese mixture on the slices of bread. Broil or bake until cheese melts. This makes approximately 30 appetizers. The unbaked pizza freezes well.

p'cha

Jellied duck giblets
A variation from the traditional calf's foot jelly

Giblets from 2 ducks (necks, hearts, stomachs, wing tips,
(no liver), cut in large bite-sized pieces.
3-4 large garlic cloves (crushed)
salt and pepper to taste (should be made quite peppery)

Place giblets in a pot with just enough water to cover. Add salt and pepper. Boil very slowly until barely tender. If water goes down in boiling, a little more may be added. Add crushed garlic and simmer about another half hour or until very tender.

Pour in a flat serving container. Liquid should just barely cover giblets. Cover with foil. Refrigerate. Enjoy, but don't get too close to anybody.

tahini dip

A flavor of Israel
Tahini is made from ground, hulled sesame seeds

8 oz canned tahini
½ C water
Juice of one large lemon
1 clove garlic, peeled and mashed
a pinch of allspice

Blend the tahini and water until it looks like thick mayonnaise. Mix in lemon juice and seasonings. Sprinkle with a little paprika for color. Serve with pita bread or crisp, raw vegetables.

hummus

A combination of tahini and chick pea paste

1 lb can of chick peas (garbanzas) drained and rinsed
1-1/3 C tahini paste from the can
1 C lemon juice
4 cloves pressed garlic
2 tsp salt

Blend all the ingredients carefully. Top with 1 TB chopped parsley for garnish, and a little cayenne pepper for color. Serve with crackers, pita bread or raw vegetables.

guacamole

Some like it hot!!! Ole!!!!

3 yellow chiles
1 tomato
1 clove garlic
2 TB onion
1 tsp salt
1 avocado

To make salsa, boil the chiles with the tomato for about 10 minutes. Remove seeds and stems from chiles. Skin tomato and place in blender. Add garlic, onion and salt and blend. Mash avocado and add salsa carefully until you have the desired strength. Serve as a dip wih tortilla chips. Salsa can also be used on steak, rice or egg.

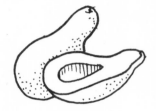

mushroom pate

1 lb firm, white mushrooms, minced
1 onion, minced
1 C water
herb bouquet (thyme, basil, oregano) tied in washed
    cheesecloth, ¼ tsp each
2 TB lemon juice
2 tsp salt
fresh ground pepper
4 eggs
½ cup cream

Set oven at 400 degrees. In saucepan, combine mushrooms, onion, water, herb bouquet, 1 TB lemon juice, salt and pepper. Cook rapidly until the water has evaporated, about 10 minutes. Remove herb bouquet. In a bowl, beat eggs and cream. Remove the mushroom mixture from the heat and add the remaining lemon juice. Taste and correct seasoning.

Add the mushroom mixture to the cream and egg mixture. Ladle the mixture into an ovenproof ramekin or Pyrex bowl. Place in a shallow pan of hot water and bake until set, about 20 minutes. Serve warm as a first course or chilled as a spread with hot buttered toast. Serves 4 as first course.

hot tuna cheese rounds

6½ oz canned tuna, drained
4 oz shredded swiss cheese
1 TB sliced green onions or scallions
½ C mayonnaise
1 TB lemon juice
1 tsp curry powder
¼ tsp salt
18 slices bread
1 7 oz can water chestnuts, diced (save some for tops)

Combine drained tuna with onion, cheese, mayonnaise, lemon juice and seasonings. Mix well. Cut bread, making 36 rounds. Place on cookie sheet. Spoon some mixture on each round. Top with a slice of water chestnut. Bake in 400 degree oven 12-15 minutes until golden and puffed.

south sea meat balls

2 tsp garlic powder
1 tsp salt
2 TB onion soup mix
1 tsp chili powder
½ tsp taco seasoning
2 lb ground beef
3 TB oil
12 oz ketchup
12 oz jar guava jelly

Mix garlic powder, salt, onion soup mix, chili powder and taco seasoning with the meat. Chop until well mixed. Form into small balls and brown in oil. Drain off fat.

Heat ketchup and guava jelly and place meat balls into the sauce. Cook for ½ hour. Keep warm until serving time on low heat or use chaffing dish. Guava jelly gives a smooth, subtle taste that will surprise you.

chopped chicken livers

The genuine heartburn classic goes modern

1 lb chicken or calf's liver
1 large onion
4 TB chicken fat
2 hard boiled eggs
salt, pepper, ginger to taste
1 TB cognac (optional)

Slice onion and saute in chicken fat until golden. Wash livers. Dry thoroughly on paper towels. Broil for a few minutes, turning once. They should not be too well done. Cut up livers, onion, eggs and place in processor. Add seasonings. Process for a few seconds, just enough to mix, but do not let it get to a paste. Place into a 2 C mold and chill. Serve with challa, rye bread or crackers.

vegetarian chicken livers

Looks and tastes like the real thing

1 C lentils
1 large onion, sauteed
4 eggs, hard boiled
2 TB maynnaise
salt, pepper, garlic salt, to taste

Soak lentils overnight in water. Add additional water, and boil for 10 minutes until soft. Drain excess water. Chop together with onions, eggs and seasonings and mayonnaise. Use processor to chop to consistency of chopped liver. Makes 4 cups.

vegetable pate

2 large onions, sliced
6 large mushrooms, sliced
1½ lbs string beans (cooked until soft)
2 eggs, hard boiled
8 walnuts, chopped fine
2-3 TB oil
salt and pepper to taste

Saute onions and mushrooms until soft, but not mushy. Chop beans and eggs together. Combine all together with walnuts, oil, salt and pepper. Processor may be used, to chop to consistency of chopped liver. Makes about 4 cups.

from barches to baguettes

BREADS AND MUFFINS

real french baguettes

50 million Frenchmen can't be wrong

1 pkg dry yeast
1½ C warm water
½ C milk
1 TB butter
1 TB sugar
2 tsp salt
5 C flour

Dissolve yeast in ¼ C warm water and set aside. In a saucepan bring milk, butter, sugar and salt to a simmer and cool. Add yeast mixture and remaining water. Add flour, 1 C at a time, blending thoroughly to make a light dough. Turn dough out onto a floured board and knead for 10 minutes or until smooth and elastic. Place dough in an oiled bowl, oil top, cover with kitchen towel and let rise in warm place for 2 hours or until double in bulk.

Divide dough into 4 parts and shape into baguettes (long loaves). Place in oiled baking pans, cover and let rise in warm place for 1 hour or until double in bulk. Cut small diagonal slits on top of loaves, brush with milk or water. Bake in 400 degree oven for 40 to 50 minutes, or until golden brown. Makes 4 baguettes.

barches

A fragrant loaf to usher in the Sabbath

1 pkg dry yeast
¼ C warm water
1 TB sugar
1 6 oz potato, boiled and mashed
    reserve potato water
2 tsp salt
2 TB oil
4 C flour

Dissolve yeast in ¼ C warm water. Add sugar and set aside until it rises. Boil potato until soft, save the potato water. Mash potatoes. Add enough potato water to the mashed potato to make 1 1/3 C. In a large bowl mix salt, oil, warm potato and water mixture and yeast. Add flour 1 C at a time. On a floured board knead for 10 minutes. Place dough in an oiled bowl, oil top, cover with wax paper and a kitchen towel and let rise in a warm place* until double in bulk. Divide into 2 parts. Knead and shape one part into 3 long rolls for braiding. Knead the first part and place in an oiled baking pan 5 x 7 x 3. Place braid on top. Let rise until double in bulk. Brush with egg yolk and sprinkle with poppy seeds. Bake at 350 degrees for 1 hour until brown and loaf sounds hollow when tapped.

*For electric ovens, turn to lowest setting for 5 minutes. Turn off. Put in yeast dough to rise. The pilot keeps gas ovens warm enough for dough to rise.

corn chili bread

3 ears fresh uncooked corn
1 C yellow cornmeal
1 tsp salt
3 tsp baking powder
1 C sour cream
¾ C melted butter
2 well beaten eggs
¼ lb finely diced Monterey Jack or Gruyere cheese
4 oz can peeled green chiles, finely chopped

Scrape the kernels from the corn and combine with rest of ingredients. Pour into a well buttered 9″ square baking dish and bake at 350 degrees for 1 hour.

award-winning bran muffins

1 large egg
1 C milk
3 TB olive oil
3 TB honey
3 TB black strap molasses
1 tsp soda
1 tsp vinegar
1 C whole wheat pastry flour
1 C bran
½ C white raisins
½ C chopped walnuts

Beat the egg and combine all the ingredients in a bowl and blend. Grease muffin pan and add the batter. Bake at 425 degrees for about 12 minutes or until done when tested with toothpick. May be frozen. Yield: 12 muffins.

dill casserole bread

4 to 4½ C flour (unbleached preferred)
¼ C sugar
1 TB salt
4 TB dill weed, dry
2 pkg dry yeast
1 C water
1 C milk
¼ C oil
1 egg

Combine 2 C flour, sugar, salt, dill weed and yeast in large mixer bowl. Heat water, milk and oil in saucepan over low heat until warm. Add egg and warm liquid to flour mixture. Blend at lowest speed of mixer until moistened. Beat three minutes at medium speed (can be beaten by hand). Stir in remaining two or two and a half cups flour to form a stiff batter, by hand.

Oil bowl and top of dough well. Cover, and let rise in warm place until light and doubled, about 1-2 hours. Stir down dough and spoon into greased 9 x 5 inch loaf pan, or into a generously greased 2-quart deep round casserole.

Bake at 375 degrees for 45-50 minutes or until loaf sounds hollow when lightly tapped. Remove immediately to cool. Brush with butter and sprinkle with coarse salt, optional.

fruity bran muffins

3 C whole bran
1 C boiling water
2 eggs, slightly beaten
2 C buttermilk
½ C salad oil
1 C raisins or chopped dates or 1 mashed banana
2½ tsp soda
½ tsp salt
2/3 C sugar
2½ C flour

Mix bran and boiling water. Cool and set aside. Add buttermilk to beaten eggs. Add salad oil and raisins. Add to bran mixture. Sift together soda, salt, sugar and flour. Stir into bran mixture, mixing only until flour dissolves. Overmixing causes tough muffins.

Bake in buttered tins at 425 degrees for 20 minutes. Makes about 30 muffins. May be frozen.

37

orange-cranberry bread

½ C slivered orange peel
1 C sugar
¼ C water
2 oz butter or margarine
1 C orange juice
2 eggs, lightly beaten
2½ C sifted flour
1 TB baking powder
½ tsp soda
1 tsp salt
¼ C wheat germ or finely chopped nuts
1 C coarsely chopped fresh cranberries
White Glaze

To prepare slivered orange peel, cut strips of peel from 4 or 5 oranges with vegetable peeler. Cut or slice peel into fine slivers. Combine sugar and water in saucepan. Add orange peel and cook, stirring occasionally, until sugar dissolves. Cook over low heat an additional 5 minutes, continuing to stir. Remove from heat. Add butter and stir until melted. Cool slightly. Add orange juice and eggs. Blend well. Sift together flour, baking powder, soda and salt. Stir in wheat germ. Add to liquid mixing only until moistened. Stir in cranberries. Pour into greased, wax paper-lined 9″ x 5″ loaf pan. Let stand 20 minutes.

Bake at 350 degrees for 1 hour and 5 minutes or until wood pick inserted in center comes out clean. Cool 10 minutes. Remove from pan and cool completely. Cover top with White Glaze, if desired. May garnish with orange slice and cranberries.

WHITE GLAZE
Stir 1½ TB milk into 1 C powdered sugar and blend till smooth.

beer bread

If you've never baked your own bread, start with this easy recipe.

3 C self-rising flour*
3 TB wheat germ, optional, but use 3 TB less flour
3 TB (scant) sugar
1 12 oz can beer NOT chilled, 6% alcohol content
1 TB sesame seeds

Sift dry ingredients into a bowl. Pour beer over all and mix until moistened with wooden spoon. Turn into 4 generously greased and floured "mini" loaf pans or a 9" x 5" loaf pan. (Using 4 small pans increases crust surface.) Level top slightly with top of spoon. Sprinkle with 1 TB sesame seeds. Bake mini loaves in 375 degree oven 30 to 35 minutes or large loaf 45 minutes. The top will not brown too much. Turn out of pans and wrap in foil to keep moist. Refrigerate or freeze and reheat in foil.

For cheese bread: Mix in 2 C grated cheddar cheese.
For onion bread: Mix in 1 C grated onion.

*Self-rising flour must be fresh and kept in an airtight container because it loses leavening power when exposed to the air. You may substitute 3 C all-purpose flour, 3 tsp baking powder and 1½ tsp sugar.

strawberry dessert bread

3 C flour
1 tsp soda
1 tsp salt
1 tsp cinnamon
2 C sugar
1 tsp vanilla
2 C fresh or frozen strawberries
4 eggs, well beaten
1¼ C oil
1¼ C chopped pecans

Sift dry ingredients into a large bowl. Make a well, mix remaining ingredients and pour into well. Stir carefully, just enough to dampen mixture. Pour into 2 9" x 5" loaf pans or 3 8½" x 3½" pans. Bake at 350 degrees for 50 minutes or 1 hour. Freezes well.

pita cheese bread

Slice pita bread open. Spread round pieces with mixture of ½ garlic spread and ½ butter or margarine. Top with grated parmesan and romano cheese. Cut round into eight triangles. Bake in 350 degree oven 10-15 minutes until bubbly and brown. Serve hot or cold.

zucchini bread

1 1/3 C flour
2/3 C sugar
½ C chopped walnuts
2¼ tsp baking powder
1 tsp grated lemon rind
2 beaten eggs
1/3 C melted margarine
1 C grated zucchini

Mix dry ingredients. Add eggs, margarine and zucchini. Bake 1 hour at 350 degrees in a 9″ x 5″ loaf pan.

COLD AND HOT SOUPS

bouillabaisse

Bring the Riviera home

¼ C olive oil
2 onions, chopped
1 leek, sliced
3 cloves garlic, minced
4 celery stalks, chopped
½ C carrots, sliced
1 lb 13 oz can tomatoes, peeled
1 tsp thyme
½ tsp fennel
2 bay leaves
3 C white wine
1 tsp salt
pepper
pinch of powdered saffron
2 lbs fish and bones for stock
2 lbs firm fish chunks

Saute onion, leek, garlic in oil until soft. Add celery, carrots, continue cooking. Add tomatoes, thyme, fennel, bay leaves, 2 C wine, salt and pepper and bring to a boil, then simmer. Add fish and simmer 1 hour. Add additional wine.

Can hold at this point, covered. Just before serving add chunks of fish and cook 10 to 15 minutes until just done. Do not over-cook. Ladle into soup bowls. Serve with Rouille for an authenic Mediterranean flavor. Serves 6.

rouille

8 garlic cloves
3 small dried red peppers
½ slice white bread, crust removed
¼ C olive oil
2 TB tomato paste
1 tsp paprika
4 to 5 drops tabasco
½ C fish stock

Use metal blade. In food processor bowl, place garlic, peppers, bread, olive oil, tomato paste, paprika, tabasco and fish stock. Process, turning on and off, for about 5 seconds, then continue processing additional 10 seconds to make a smooth paste, adding more fish stock if necessary. For hotter rouille, add more tabasco. Serve with bouillabaise.

cabbage meatball borscht

For that cold rainy day

1 medium head of cabbage
½ tsp salt
1 large onion diced
2 large carrots sliced thin or shredded
1 can (28 oz) tomatoes cut into small pieces
1 can (8 oz) tomato sauce plus 1 can water
6 TB brown sugar
2 TB lemon juice
1 lb ground beef
1 egg
2 TB brown sugar
1 TB lemon juice
1 slice white bread
1 tsp salt
½ tsp garlic powder
¼ tsp black pepper

Cut cabbage in quarters. Wash and core. Slice cabbage as if for cole slaw. Put cut cabbage in large pot. Add salt and mix throughly. Add onion, carrots, tomatoes, tomato sauce, water, brown sugar and lemon juice. Bring to a boil stirring occasionally.

While the soup is coming to a boil put the ground beef in a large mixing bowl. In a blender combine all the remaining ingredients. Blend until smooth. Add to the ground beef and mix well. Make 24 meatballs. Add to the boiling soup. Lower flame to simmer and cook for 1 hour or until meatballs are done and the cabbage is tender.

beef barley soup

You'll remember Mama

3 lb soup bones, chuck and flanken
½ C barley
1 onion, whole
1 parsnip, whole
sprig of parsley
1 clove garlic
4 stalks celery, cut up
½ tsp dill weed
salt and white pepper, to taste
3 potatoes, diced
4 carrots, peeled and diced
1 1-lb can peas or 1 pkg frozen, optional

Cover meat with water in a large kettle. Bring to a boil and skim top. To keep soup white and creamy, add barley slowly while soup is boiling. Add onion, parsnip, parsley, garlic, celery, dill weed and salt and pepper. Cook for 1½ hours. Add carrots and potatoes and simmer until meat and vegetables are tender. Add peas last, if you use them, about 5 minutes before serving time. Remove onion, parsnip and parsley. Adjust seasonings. If soup gets too thick, thin with a small amount of hot water. Serve with chunks of meat in each bowl.

asparagus soup

A springtime treat

2 lbs asparagus
2 TB margarine
1 onion, chopped
4 C chicken broth
salt, pepper and nutmeg to taste
1 TB chopped parsley for garnish

Wash asparagus and slice, keeping the tips aside. In a frying pan saute onion in margarine until soft. Add asparagus stalks and cook 3 minutes. Add broth, salt and pepper and nutmeg. Simmer about 15 minutes, or until stalks are tender. Add tips and cook until tender. Remove tips.

Puree cooked mixture in processor, about 2 cups at a time. Serve hot, garnished with tips, and chopped parsley. Serves 4-6. May be prepared ahead of time, and reheated.

chicken barley soup

1 4 to 5 lb chicken, reserve chicken breast
2 chicken bouillon cubes, dissolved in hot water
          or
1 can chicken broth
1/3 C barley
1 onion, whole
1 parsnip, whole
1 clove garlic
3 carrots, peeled and sliced
3 stalks celery, cut up
½ tsp dill weed or snip of fresh dill
salt and white pepper to taste
peas, optional

Cut up and wash chicken, reserving breast for later. Cover with water and add bouillon cubes or broth. Bring to a boil and skim top. Add barley slowly while soup boils. Add onion, parsnip, garlic, celery, dill, salt and pepper. Simmer for an hour. Add carrots and chicken breast and cook for twenty minutes. Cut up the white meat and serve with each bowl of soup. If chicken is tough, longer cooking will be necessary.

schav*

The three "zoiers" (sours) beet borscht, cabbage borscht and schav were the mainstays of the Eastern European diet

6 C water
1 large onion, quartered
1 large potato, peeled and sliced
salt and pepper
1 lb fresh spinach or 1-10 oz pkg frozen
3 TB lemon juice
2 TB sugar
½ pt sour cream
1 hard boiled egg

Place water, onion, potato, salt and pepper in a saucepan. Bring to a boil, then simmer until potato is nearly done. Add the spinach, lemon and sugar. Bring to a boil, then simmer for 10 minutes. Adjust seasonings.

Place in processor or blender for 1 minute. Chill for several hours. Serve with sour cream and slices of hard boiled egg.

*Sorrel leaves or sour grass are not available in Southern California. Spinach with the sour taste of lemon makes a delicious substitute.

beet borscht

Try making it from scratch

2 bunches beets, with greens (about 8 medium beets)
1 onion
1 can stewed tomatoes (about 1 lb)
juice of 2 lemons
½ C sugar
salt to taste

Scrub beets, don't peel: save greens. Put beets in pot with peeled onion and cover with 3 to 4 quarts water. Simmer till beets are tender about 1½ hours, remove them and chop. Discard onion and return beets to water. Add greens, washed and chopped, and the canned tomatoes, also chopped.

Add lemon juice, sugar, and salt, adjusting to taste. Cook until greens are tender, about 20 minutes. Chill and serve with sour cream dollops.

And Esau said to Jacob: "Give me some of that red stuff to gulp down, for I am famished."

Genesis 25:30

beet borscht
Quick and easy

1 16 oz can beets
1 quart buttermilk
1 cucumber peeled and sliced (1½ C)
1 bunch green onions (use white part only)
salt and pepper to taste
¼ tsp citric acid
1 TB lemon juice
1 TB sugar

Place all ingredients in a blender or processor. Blend until smooth. Chill a few hours to blend flavors. Serves 6.

tuna chowder

¾ C green onions, chopped
¼ C celery, diced
3 TB butter
3 C diced raw potatoes
2½ C water
1½ tsp salt
1½ TB flour
2 C milk, skim milk may be used
16 oz creamed corn
16 oz canned tomatoes, quartered, drained
13 oz white tuna, rinsed and drained
½ tsp garlic powder
½ tsp marjoram
½ tsp rosemary
¼ tsp white pepper
1 pkg frozen peas (optional)

Saute onions and celery in butter for 5 minutes. Add potatoes, water and salt. Heat to boiling, and cook over medium heat for 15 minutes.

In a small dish blend flour and ¼ C milk. Stir into potato mixture, adding remainder of milk. Cook until thick. Add corn, tomatoes, tuna, garlic powder, marjoram, rosemary, pepper and peas. Add more salt if desired. Cook until everything is heated thoroughly.

broccoli soup

¼ C salad oil
1 onion, diced
1 large potato, diced
2/3 C celery, diced
1 garlic clove, minced
½ tsp pepper
3 C chopped broccoli or 1-10 oz pkg frozen
      chopped broccoli, thawed
5 C chicken broth
¼ C fresh chopped basil or 1 TB dried basil

In a large saucepan, heat oil. Add onion and saute until tender, about 10 minutes. Add potato, celery, garlic, pepper. Cook 10 minutes stirring occasionally. Add broccoli, broth and basil. Cover and simmer 20 minutes. Into blender container, pour half of soup. Blend smooth. Repeat with rest of soup. Adjust seasonings. Reheat and serve.

For cream soup use vegetable broth. After blending, reheat and serve with cream or sour cream. Makes 6 cups.

cream of vegetable soup

This is a colorful tasty soup

2 C vegetable broth
1 C diced raw potato
½ C sliced celery
½ C chopped onion
½ C shredded or sliced carrot
1 C coarsely shredded or sliced cabbage
2 TB butter or margarine, melted
2 TB flour
1½ C milk

Combine broth, potato, celery, onion and carrot in a 2 qt saucepan. Bring to a boil, simmer 15 minutes. Add cabbage and simmer 5 additional minutes.

In a saucepan melt butter or margarine, stir in flour and cook until smooth, stirring constantly. Remove from heat, gradually stir in milk. Boil, stirring constantly for 1 minute. Add to cooked vegetable mixture. Heat to serving temperature. *Do not boil!* Season with salt and pepper (white) to taste. Garnish with dill weed.

gazpacho

From Mazatlan, Cuernavaca, Veracruz, ver vayst . . . who knows

2 medium tomatoes, quartered
1 onion, peeled, quartered
1 green pepper, quartered and seeded
1 cucumber, peeled, cut in chunks
4 C tomato juice
2 TB wine vinegar
1 tsp salt
dash cayenne or hot pepper sauce
3 TB olive oil
½ tsp oregano, crushed
freshly ground pepper to taste
2-3 cloves garlic (optional)

Put vegetables into processor container ½ filled and process until smooth. Pour into large bowl. Add juice and seasonings. Stir and chill.

GARNISH
1 cucumber
1 stalk celery
½ C jicama
croutons
1 onion
1 green pepper
1 tomato

Before serving, coarsely chop vegetables one at a time. Add to soup. Add croutons and serve. Serves 10-12.

split pea soup

4 or 5 soup bones
4 qts water
2½ C dried split peas, soak 4 to 5 hours or overnight
3 leeks, cut into small pieces
5 stalks celery, diced
5 carrots, peeled and diced
1 onion diced
½ bunch parsley
4 cloves garlic
½ tsp each oregano, rosemary, chervil
salt and pepper to taste
2 potatoes (optional)
¼ C lemon juice to taste

Cook soup bones in large kettle of water and skim top as it boils. Add all the above ingredients and simmer for 4 hours. Put about ½ of the soup in a blender and liquefy. Mix together with the rest of the soup and season with lemon juice, about ¼ C. Adjust seasonings and serve with sourdough bread.

lentil soup

2 C dry lentils
2½ qt water
2-3 lbs veal knuckles
2 carrots, cut in pieces
1 large onion, quartered
1 stalk celery, cut in pieces
1 clove garlic
2 bay leaves
1 TB crushed thyme
1 TB salt
½ tsp freshly ground pepper
½-¾ lb smoked sausage

In large kettle combine lentils, water, veal knuckles, carrots, onion, celery, garlic, bay leaves, thyme, salt and pepper. Bring to boil, reduce heat and simmer, covered, until lentils are soft and tender, about 1½ hours. Strain, reserving liquid. Discard bones.

Puree lentil mixture in blender or food processor and pour into reserved liquid. Place over low heat and add sliced sausage. Simmer, covered for about 40-45 minutes. Makes approximately 3 quarts.

chicken gumbo soup

Gumbo comes from the French "gombo" which means okra.
This is one "authentic" version.

Israelis prepare fresh okra by washing and drying
in the sun for ½ hour to take off the shine.

16 chicken parts
salt and pepper to taste
flour to dredge chicken
4 TB oil
1 C chopped onion
1 C chopped celery
1 C chopped green pepper
2 cloves mashed garlic
6 C water
½ tsp cayenne pepper
1 tsp file, optional (available in fish markets)
2 C fresh or canned okra

Season chicken with salt and pepper and dredge in flour. Brown chicken in oil. Remove from pan. Saute until limp and golden, onion, celery, green pepper and garlic. Add water, and cayenne pepper. Add chicken. Cover, bring to a boil, then simmer for 1 hour.*

Add okra and file. Simmer 10 minutes more if fresh, and 4 minutes if canned. Serve over rice. Serves 6-8.

*May be prepared ahead to this point.
  Chilled to remove the fat, and then reheated with okra.

creamed corn soup

1½ C chicken broth or ½ lb chicken backs
17 oz can creamed corn
salt and pepper to taste
1 TB cornstarch (optional)
2 TB water (optional)
1 scallion, finely chopped for garnish

Cook chicken in enough water to cover. Season with salt and pepper. After 25 minutes remove chicken, cool, debone and shred. You should have about 1½ C broth.

Heat the broth, creamed corn and shredded chicken together. Make a paste with cornstarch and water. Add to soup to desired consistency. Serve, garnished with scallion. Serves 4.

51

low calorie cream of mushroom soup

CREAM SOUP BASE
1 C low-fat cottage cheese or ricotta cheese*
1 C low-fat milk

Combine cheese and milk in blender and whirl until smooth.

*Ricotta cheese will produce a creamier consistency.

CREAM OF MUSHROOM
2 TB oil
½-¾ lb sliced mushrooms
1 small onion, thinly sliced
1 recipe Cream Soup Base
2 cups vegetable broth
salt to taste
freshly grated nutmeg
freshly chopped parsley

Heat oil in heavy 3 or 4 qt saucepan over medium heat. Add mushrooms and onion and cook, stirring frequently, until onion is soft. Remove from heat and allow to cool slightly. Stir in soup base and stock.

Transfer to blender jar and whirl until smooth. Return to burner and cook gently over low heat just to heat through, but *do not boil* or it will curdle. Season to taste with salt. Serve hot or cold, garnished with a sprinkling of freshly grated nutmeg and parsley, if desired.

Makes 4-6 servings.

hearty vegetable soup provencale

Feeds a mob

Into an 8 qt pot combine

        4 qt water
        3 TB salt
        2 C potatoes diced
        2 C onions, sliced thin
        ½ C celery, chopped
        ½ head cabbage, chopped

Boil for 40 minutes.

15 minutes before serving add:

        1 lb frozen zucchini
        1 lb frozen Italian green beans
        1 lb frozen peas and carrots
        1 lb can chick peas, drained
        1 lb can kidney beans, drained
        4 oz broken spaghetti
        ¼ tsp pepper
        1 tsp salt
        pinch saffron
        1 slice stale bread, crumbled

In a separate small bowl mix:

        6 cloves garlic mashed
        1 6-oz can tomato paste
        1½ TB dried basil or 2 leaves fresh, chopped
        ¾ C grated fresh parmesan cheese
        Add ¼ C olive oil DROP BY DROP

Beat into soup just before serving, adjust seasonings.

forest mushroom soup

Elusive and exotic

1 oz dry forest mushrooms (oriental "shiitake")
4 tsp beef flavor base
6 C water
1 large bunch green onions, chopped
3 TB margarine or butter
1 clove garlic mashed
1 TB lemon juice
> or
½ C Madeira wine or dry sherry
1 TB chopped parsley
thinly sliced raw mushrooms for garnish (optional)

Soak forest mushrooms in enough water to cover for ½ hour. Remove stems. Discard soaking water.

Heat beef flavor base in 6 C water. Add soaked mushrooms. Bring to a boil. Simmer for ½ hour. Saute onions and garlic in butter for 5 minutes. Add to soup. Flavor with lemon juice and garnish with thin lemon slices. Or, add Madeira wine and garnish with chopped parsley. You may add sliced raw mushrooms for garnish. Serves 6.

tomato soup

You'll never get this taste from a can

4 TB margarine
4 TB flour
6 TB tomato paste
4 C chicken broth
1 tsp salt
½ tsp pepper
4 tsp sugar
½ tsp oregano

Melt margarine in saucepan and add flour. Over medium heat stir continuously until roux is brown. Add ½ C chicken broth and stir until smooth. Then add all the tomato paste and mix well. Finish pouring the chicken broth into mixture. Add salt, pepper, sugar and oregano and bring to a boil. Turn heat down and simmer for 15-20 minutes. If you wish a thinner soup, add more chicken soup.

from quiche to kugel

NOODLE, RICE AND CHEESE CASSEROLES

blintz pie

Serve in a pretty round tart pan

¼ lb butter
3 TB sugar
2 eggs
¾ C milk
1¼ C flour
1 tsp baking powder
1 lb hoop cheese
2 TB butter, melted
1 egg
1 tsp sugar
pinch of salt
1 TB sour cream

Beat butter, sugar, eggs, milk, flour and baking powder together. Pour into greased 9″ baking pan in which pie will be served. Mix together hoop cheese, butter, egg, sugar, salt and sour cream. Spread on top of batter. Bake at 350 degrees for 1 hour.

Serve hot with sour cream and jelly. May be put together a day ahead and refrigerated and baked before serving. It is best served hot.

cheese potato bake

1 lb potatoes, grated
1 C milk
1 C grated Gruyere cheese
1 small onion, minced
1 egg lightly beaten
2 TB melted butter
1 tsp salt
dash pepper

Combine all the above ingredients and put in a buttered 1½ qt dish. Bake covered for 1 hour in a 350 degree oven. Uncover and bake for 30 minutes more or until golden.

beer and cheddar quiche

1 9" unbaked pastry shell
    or 8 4" shells
2 C shredded sharp cheddar cheese
2 TB flour
½ tsp salt
dash of cayenne pepper
½ tsp dry mustard
¼ C imitation bacon bits
4 eggs, beaten
1 C milk
½ C beer
1½ TB instant onion flakes

Toss cheddar cheese with flour, salt, mustard and pepper. Mix bits, eggs, milk, beer and onions together. Add to cheese mixture. Pour into pastry shell.

Bake 9" shell 40-45 minutes at 350 degrees. Bake 4" shells 30 minutes at 350 degrees. Let stand 10 minutes before serving. 6 to 8 servings.

chili cheese souffle

¼ lb butter
10 eggs
½ C flour
1 tsp baking powder
¼ tsp salt
1 7 oz can green chilis, chopped
1 pt cottage cheese
1 lb Jack cheese

Melt butter in a 9 x 13 pan or pyrex dish. Beat the eggs in a large bowl, add flour, baking powder and salt and blend. Add melted butter, chilis, cottage cheese and Jack cheese, and mix until blended. Turn batter into pan and bake at 400 degrees for 15 minutes. Reduce heat to 350 degrees and bake 35-40 minutes longer. Cut into squares. Serves 12 as a side dish, or cut into smaller squares and serve as a hot hors d'oeuvre.

cottage enchiladas

1 C dairy sour cream
1½ C cottage cheese
1 C chopped green onion
1 tsp salt
⅛ tsp pepper
1 7 oz can whole green chiles
10 corn tortillas
¼ C oil
1 small pkg enchilada sauce mix, 1⅝ oz
1 large can red chili sauce, 1 lb 12 oz
¾ lb Jack cheese, cut in strips
¾ lb extra-sharp cheddar cheese, cut in strips

Blend sour cream, cottage cheese, chopped green onions, seasoned salt and pepper.

Remove seeds from chiles and cut in strips. Saute tortillas in oil a few seconds on each side to soften. Drain on paper towels. Mix the dry enchilada sauce mix with the can of red chili sauce and pour some on bottom of oblong baking dish.

Place about 2 spoonfuls of cottage cheese mixture, plus the two cheeses on each open tortilla, reserving remaining cheese mixture for garnish. Reserve 1/3 of the Jack and cheddar cheeses and chili strips for garnish. Divide remaining among 10 tortillas.

Roll filled tortillas and arrange in baking dish. Pour remaining enchilada sauce mixture over all. Cover baking dish with foil and bake at 350 degrees for 30 minutes or until very hot.

Just before serving, spoon reserved cottage cheese mixture over top plus the reserved chile. Broil until cheese is bubbly. Makes 5 to 10 servings.

broccoli cheese bake

1 lb fresh broccoli, or 1 package frozen
¼ tsp garlic powder or ¼ tsp curry powder
3 eggs
1 tsp seasoned salt
¼ lb jack cheese, shredded
¼ lb sharp cheddar cheese, shredded

Cook broccoli until just soft. Put into a 8″ x 8″ pan. Sprinkle with garlic powder. Beat eggs with seasoned salt and pour over broccoli. Pour shredded cheeses over mixture. Bake at 350 degrees for 40 minutes.

real italian spaghetti sauce

From a well seasoned Italian friend

¼ C imported olive oil*
1 large clove garlic, chopped fine
1 35 oz can imported, crushed, Italian plum
    tomatoes with basil
¼ C fresh parsley, chopped
¼ tsp fennel seeds
1 small bay leaf
2 sprigs fresh basil leaves or ½ tsp dried
salt and pepper to taste

In a deep saucepan, heat oil, add garlic and brown lightly. Add crushed tomatoes and heat to boiling. Bubble gently for 5 minutes. Add parsley, fennel seeds, bay leaf, basil, salt and pepper. Simmer for 2 hours, stirring frequently.

*For that authentic Italian flavor, use all the best imported ingredients.

souper rice

1 C rice, converted or regular
1 can chicken broth, undiluted
1 can chicken gumbo soup, undiluted
1 jar sliced mushrooms, drained, or ½ lb fresh mushrooms
    sauteed in margarine
1 onion, chopped, sauteed in margarine

Combine all ingredients in a pan. Bring to a boil on top of stove. Bake in 350 degree oven for 45 minutes.

mexican casserole

1 onion, chopped
2 TB oil
1 1 lb 12 oz can tomatoes
1 envelope taco seasoning mix
½ tsp seasoned salt
1 4 oz can chopped green chiles, optional
1 6 oz pkg tortilla chips
1 lb Jack cheese, shredded
1 C sour cream
½ C shredded cheddar cheese

Saute onions in oil until tender. Add tomatoes, taco mix, salt and green chiles. Simmer uncovered, 10 to 15 minutes. In a buttered, deep 2 qt casserole, arrange half of tortilla chips, sauce and Jack cheese in layers. Repeat layers and top with sour cream.

Bake at 325 degrees for 30 minutes. Sprinkle with cheddar cheese and bake 10 minutes longer. Let stand 15 minutes before cutting into squares. Serves 6 to 8.

swiss cheese noodle bake

8 oz medium noodles, cooked, drained, hot
½ lb swiss cheese grated
1 TB onion juice
1 tsp Worcestershire sauce
¼ C melted butter or margarine
½ tsp salt
¼ tsp pepper
1 pt sour cream
½ C buttered bread crumbs

Boil noodles and drain. Add cheese to noodles while still hot, and toss to mix lightly. Add onion juice, Worcestershire sauce, butter, salt and pepper. Cool. Combine with sour cream, mix lightly but thoroughly. Place in buttered casserole and top with buttered bread crumbs. Bake in 350 degree oven 1 hour.

orange and apple noodle kugel

Everybody loves a kugel, especially this one

16 oz wide egg noodles
¼ lb butter or margarine
8 eggs
3 C orange juice
juice and pulp of 1 orange
1 C sugar scant
1 tsp salt
1 tsp vanilla (optional)
2 tart apples grated
2 tsp lemon juice
cinnamon, sugar and nuts for topping, optional

Cook noodles, and toss with melted butter. Beat eggs, add orange juice, sugar, salt, pulp of orange. Pour over noodles.

Mix grated apples and lemon juice and add to noodles and mix. Pour into 9 x 13 greased pan. You may sprinkle top with cinnamon, sugar and nuts. Bake in 350 degree oven for 1 hour.

meatless stuffed manicotti

The flavor of Italy

12 manicotti shells
1½ C cottage cheese
2 TB matzo meal
1 egg beaten
1 10 oz package frozen chopped spinach,
    cooked and drained
1 tsp seasoned salt
½ tsp Italian seasonings (basil, oregano)
3 TB grated parmesan cheese
1 tsp dried minced onion
1 15 oz jar meatless spaghetti sauce with
    onions and peppers
1/3 C water to rinse spaghetti sauce jar
1 C shredded cheddar cheese
1 C sliced mushrooms (optional)

Cook manicotti shells in 2 quarts of salted water about 7 minutes, or until almost tender. Drain and rinse in cold water, handling carefully.*

Combine cottage cheese, matzo meal, egg, spinach, seasonings, parmesan cheese and onion. Stuff the shells with cheese and spinach mixture.

Arrange in a lightly greased baking dish. Top with spaghetti sauce, then cheddar cheese and sliced mushrooms. Bake at 375 degrees 30 minutes until bubbly and brown. Serves 6.

*Some manicotti products recommend a quicker one step method without precooking the manicotti. Follow the directions on the package using 2 16 oz jars of spaghetti sauce diluted with 10 oz water.

salmon "quiche"

No crust

2 TB butter or margarine
1 lb mixed fresh vegetables: green onions,
    celery, green pepper, bean sprouts,
    water chestnuts*
1 7¾ oz can salmon or tuna, drained
4 oz swiss cheese, shredded
4 eggs
1½ C half and half
1 tsp salt
¼ tsp pepper
1 tsp dry mustard
2 tsp Worcestershire sauce
1 TB lemon juice
1 TB flour

Saute onion, celery, green pepper in butter until soft. Add bean sprouts and water chestnuts. Spread this mixture into a greased 6 C baking dish. Top with chunks of salmon. Sprinkle cheese over all.

Beat eggs, half and half together. Add salt, pepper, mustard, Worchestershire sauce, lemon juice and flour. Mix well and pour over quiche.

Bake at 375 degrees for 40 minutes until puffed and brown and custard is set. Serve hot. Serves 4-6.

*Can be found packaged together in the produce department of your market.

spinach cheese bake

6 eggs
6 TB flour
10 oz package frozen spinach, defrosted and drained
8 oz sharp cheddar cheese, shredded
¼ lb melted butter
⅛ tsp nutmeg

Beat eggs and flour together with an electric beater until smooth. Add spinach, cheese, butter and nutmeg. Place in 1½ quart bowl or souffle dish.

Bake in 350 degree oven for 1 hour, or until knife inserted in center comes out clean. Good hot or cold.

tomato cheese strata

A variation of an old favorite

10 slices egg bread
1 lb swiss cheese, grated
2 lbs canned tomatoes
6 TB minced onions
6 TB hot water
½ lb mushrooms
2 tsp dried basil
4 eggs
1½ C milk
salt and pepper to taste
4 TB parmesan cheese, grated

Butter slices of bread on one side. Trim crusts. Crowd together, butter side down in a 9 x 13 greased casserole. Use crusts to fill spaces if necessary. One layer only.

Sprinkle grated swiss cheese over bread. Drain tomatoes well, even the juice in the tomatoes. Chop into pieces. Scatter over cheese. Soak the minced onions in hot water. Scatter over tomatoes. Saute mushrooms in small amount of butter. Drain and scatter over all. Sprinkle basil over this.

Beat eggs with milk and salt and pepper. Pour over all. Sprinkle with parmesan cheese. Place in refrigerator overnight. Pre-heat oven to 350 degrees and bake for 45 minutes to 1 hour. The top should be dry. You may turn off the oven and let it sit for an extra few minutes to dry. Serves 8-10.

spinach cheese kugel

Everybody's favorite

16 oz pkg noodles
3 eggs
1 pt sour cream
1 envelope onion soup mix
1 pkg chopped spinach, defrosted
4 oz cheddar cheese, grated

Cook noodles according to package directions. Meanwhile, beat eggs and add sour cream, onion soup mix, drained spinach. Beat together. Drain noodles, add egg mixture to noodles and mix well. Sprinkle cheddar cheese on top. Bake in 9 x 13 casserole at 350 degrees for one hour. Allow to set 10 minutes before cutting.

tuna lasagna

Gets better with each layer

12-14 oz tuna solid pack, albacore, white
¾ C onion, chopped
½ C celery, chopped
1 clove garlic, minced
2 TB parsley, finely chopped
2 oz butter or margarine, melted
1 can (28 oz) tomatoes
½ C water
6 oz tomato paste
1 TB sugar
dash pepper
½ tsp oregano
1 tsp bay leaf, crushed
1 tsp sweet basil, crushed
1 tsp salt
8 oz lasagna noodles
1 pint cottage cheese (small curd)
2 eggs
½ C grated parmesan cheese
½ lb grated mozzarella cheese

Drain tuna thoroughly and rinse, and break into pieces. Cook onion, celery, garlic and parsley in butter until tender. Add tomatoes, water, tomato paste, sugar, pepper, oregano, bayleaf, basil and salt. Cook noodles as directed on package. There should be 9 noodles. In a bowl combine cottage cheese, eggs and tuna.

Cover bottom of 3 quart (8¾″ x 13½″) casserole with a thin layer of sauce, then layer:

3 cooked noodles
½ tuna mixture
½ parmesan cheese
3 noodles
thin layer of sauce
remaining tuna mixture
remaining parmesan cheese
3 noodles
remaining sauce
Mozzarella cheese

Bake uncovered for 30 minutes at 350 degrees until hot and bubbly. Let stand for a few minutes before serving. Serves 8.

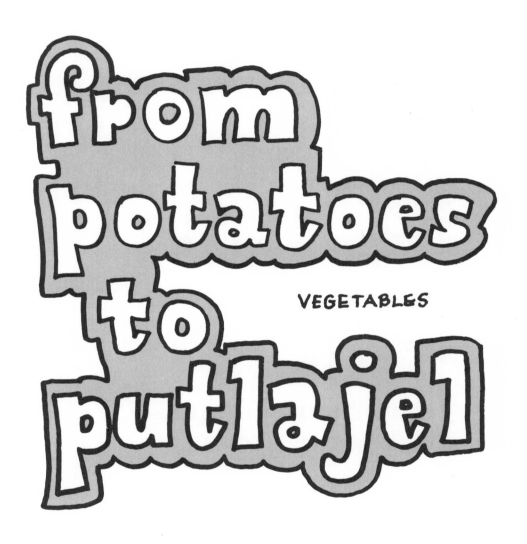

from potatoes to putlajel

VEGETABLES

asparagus polanaise

Could have been Chopin's favorite

1½ lbs asparagus
½ C butter
¼ C soft bread crumbs
1 egg, hard boiled and chopped
1 TB finely chopped parsley
salt and pepper to taste

Cook asparagus until just tender. Melt the butter. When it foams, stir in the bread crumbs and continue to cook over low heat until the crumbs are well browned.

Remove from heat and stir in the egg, parsley and salt and pepper. Place asparagus in a heated platter. Cover with crumb mixture and serve at once.

beets in mustard sauce

1½ C canned sliced beets, drained (10oz can)
2 oz red onions, thinly sliced
½ C plain yogurt
1 TB mustard (Dijon, or French prepared)
2 tsp white vinegar
½ tsp whole cloves
salt and pepper to taste

Combine beets and onions in a bowl. In a separate bowl combine yogurt, mustard, vinegar, cloves and salt and pepper. Pour over beet and onion mixture. Toss to blend and chill.

green bean saute

1 lb green beans, cut in thirds, diagonally
4 TB margarine
1 or 2 cloves minced garlic
1/3 C parmesan cheese

Drop beans into rapidly boiling salted water and cook until just tender. Rinse immediately with cold water and drain well. Melt margarine in a large frying pan with the garlic. Add beans and stir to coat evenly. Take off heat. Add the parmesan, and toss well. Serve at once.

mexican corn pudding

2 eggs, beaten
1 lb can creamed style corn
1 C yellow corn meal
1½ C grated cheddar cheese (sharp)
¾ C milk
½ tsp salt
½ C oil
½ tsp soda
2 TB chopped Ortega chili
1 TB chopped pimiento
¼ bell pepper chopped
sour cream, optional

Save small amount of cheese for top of casserole. Mix all ingredients together. Put in 1½ qt greased casserole. Bake at 350 degrees for 45 minutes. Serve with sour cream if desired.

carrots and acorn squash

2 acorn squash, cut in half and seeded
5 carrots, peeled and sliced
salt and pepper, to taste
1 egg
2 TB brown sugar
butter or margarine
½ tsp maple flavoring
2 TB yogurt, plain

Cut squash in two and remove seeds. Place in oven on a baking pan. Bake at 350 degrees for 1 hour. When tender remove from oven. Cook carrots until soft. Scoop out the squash from the shells and mash with the carrots. Add egg, brown sugar, flavoring, yogurt, salt and pepper. Stuff the acorn shell and reheat in oven when ready to serve.

carrot ring

1 C shortening
½ C brown sugar
2 whole eggs
1 TB water
1 TB orange juice
2 C grated carrots
1½ C flour
½ tsp baking soda
1 tsp baking powder
½ tsp salt
½ tsp cinnamon
½ tsp nutmeg

Mix all ingredients together. Pour into greased 1 qt ring mold. Set in refrigerator overnight or for 5 to 6 hours. When ready to bake, remove from refrigerator ½ hour before baking. Bake 1 hour at 350 degrees. When ready to serve, turn out into a large round platter. Fill center with Chinese peas or with other peas.

carrots and apricots

1 lb pkg frozen carrots
1 6 oz pkg dried apricots
1 12 oz can apricot nectar
2 TB brown sugar
butter or margarine to dot the top

Soak carrots and apricots in apricot nectar overnight. Mix with brown sugar. Place in greased 1½ qt baking dish. Dot the top with butter. Bake at 350 degrees 35 minutes. Serves 8.

carrots and applesauce

8 carrots peeled and cut into ¼ inch slices
2 TB butter
3 TB brown sugar
½ C applesauce

Cook carrots in a small amount of salted water until tender. Drain thoroughly. Melt butter and add brown sugar. Stir until sugar is dissolved. Add applesauce and the butter and sugar mixture to the carrots. Stir until carrots are evenly coated. Heat until warmed through. Serve.

dilly lime carrots

1½ lbs carrots, peeled, diagonally sliced,
    or left whole if small, cooked and drained
¼ C butter or margarine
1 tsp grated lime peel
1 TB lime juice
1 tsp instant minced onion or grated onion
½ tsp dried dill weed
2 TB coarsely chopped peanuts

Melt butter in a small saucepan. Add lime peel, juice, onion and dill. Heat well. Arrange cooked carrots in a serving dish. Pour mixture over. Sprinkle with nuts. Serves 4-6.

sesame eggplant

Wash and dry eggplant. Slice lengthwise into ⅛" thick slices. Spread each slice with mayonnaise. Sprinkle with sesame seeds. Place on cookie sheet. Bake in 325 degree oven for about 20 minutes.

eggplant neopolitan

2 large eggplants
2 eggs beaten lightly
½ TB crumpled basil
1 lb ricotta cheese
¼ lb grated Jack cheese
½ C grated parmesan cheese
1 15 oz can tomato sauce with tomato bits
2 frozen spinach souffles, baked ½ hour

Peel and slice eggplant into ¼" thick slices. Put into paper sack with flour, salt and pepper and shake. Fry in oil on low flame until golden brown. Drain on paper towels.

Mix eggs, basil, cheeses in mixmaster until blended. Grease 3 qt 9" x 13" pyrex pan. Layer tomato sauce, eggplant, cheese, tomato sauce again and top with spinach souffle.

Bake in 375 degree oven for 30 minutes. May be frozen, defrosted and rebaked for 20 minutes. Serves 8 vegetarians for main dish, or 12 as vegetable.

eggplant portugaise

1 medium eggplant
¼ lb margarine
½ onion, chopped
½ C chicken broth
½ clove garlic, minced
pinch oregano
salt, pepper
1 large tomato
1 TB chopped parsley

Peel eggplant and cut into small cubes. Melt margarine in skillet, add onion and cook until tender but not brown. Add eggplant and stir. Add chicken broth, cover and simmer 2 to 3 minutes. Add garlic, oregano, pinch salt and pepper. Mix, cover and simmer 3 to 4 minutes. Peel and dice tomato very fine. Add to eggplant the last 2 minutes of cooking. Add parsley, mix and serve hot or cold. Serves 4.

colache

Fresh vegetable stew

2 TB vegetable oil
1 C finely chopped onions
1 tsp finely chopped garlic
2 lbs zucchini or yellow squash, thoroughly
    scrubbed but not peeled, cut crosswise into
    ¼ inch thick slices
1 lb fresh green string beans, trimmed, washed and
    cut crosswise into 1½ inch length
1 tsp finely chopped fresh hot green chilies
    (more can be used, depending on taste)
4 medium firm ripe tomatoes, peeled, seeded and
    coarsely chopped, or 1 lb can whole tomatoes, drained
2 tsp salt
¼ tsp freshly ground black pepper
1 C fresh corn kernels, cut from 2 large ears of corn

In a heavy 7-8 quart casserole, heat the oil over moderate heat until a light haze forms above it. Add onions and garlic and stirring frequently, cook for about 5 minutes, until they are soft and translucent.

Add string beans, cook over low heat, stirring about 10 minutes. Add zucchini and chilies, cook about 3 minutes. Add tomatoes, salt and pepper. Cover and simmer about 10 minutes. Add corn and continue to cook until all are cooked, but still crisp to the bite. Do not overcook. Serve immediately. Serves 8 as a side dish.

A good mixture of vegetables cooked in their own juices.

candied sweet potatoes

Never fail

4 lbs sweet potatoes or yams (yams are better)
½ lb butter or margarine
½ lb brown (dark) sugar

Parboil potatoes in the jackets in salted water until they are almost tender but not too soft. When they have cooled, peel the skins and cut in half lengthwise. Place in a baking dish or an oven proof serving dish ready for the sauce.

Combine the sugar and butter in a pot and cook and stir until the mixture thickens and has turned to butterscotch. Pour over the potatoes. Then heat in a 350 degree oven for about ½ hour. Turn off heat. Let stand in oven until ready to serve. Delicious and very easy.

sweet potato pudding

3 C sweet potatoes, boiled, peeled and
    sliced or mashed (2 lbs fresh or 2½ lbs canned)
    yams may be used, they are less starchy and
    have fewer calories
2 C thin apple slices, peeled
1 C chopped blanched almonds
1/3 C orange juice
¾ C brown sugar
1 tsp grated lemon rind
2 tsp melted butter or margarine
¼ tsp cinnamon
a pinch of salt

Mix together juice, sugar, lemon rind, butter, cinnamon and salt. Alternate layers of
potatoes, apples and almonds in a 2 qt casserole and pour juice mixture in between.
Bake in 350 degree oven for 50 minutes.

squash casserole

1½ C cracker crumbs
2 lbs grated summer squash or yellow crookneck
4 TB flour
1 TB baking powder
3 eggs beaten
½ C chicken stock or milk
1 minced garlic clove
1 grated onion
salt and pepper to taste
2 TB margarine

Grease 2 qt casserole. Sprinkle with ¼ C crumbs. Mix squash, flour, baking powder, eggs, stock, garlic, onion, salt and pepper. Layer squash and remaining crumbs alternately in casserole ending with crumbs. Dot top with margarine. Bake at 350 degrees 30 minutes.

devilled brussels sprouts

2 C brussels sprouts
½ C butter or margarine
2 TB minced onion
1 TB prepared mustard
½ tsp salt
1 tsp Worchestershire sauce
dash of cayenne pepper

Cook sprouts until tender-crisp. Melt the butter in a suacepan. Add onions and cook until soft but not brown. Blend in mustard, salt and pepper and Worcestershire sauce. Drain sprouts. Place in a heated serving dish. Pour sauce over and serve at once.

zucchini casserole trio

ZUCCHINI-TOMATO
¾ lb zucchini
1 lb tomatoes fresh or canned
4 large slices stale white bread, crusts removed
4 TB melted butter
salt and pepper
1 heaping TB chopped fresh basil
            or
1 tsp sugar
¼ lb cheese sliced thin, mozzarella, gruyere or cheddar

Slice unpeeled zucchini very thin and sprinkle with salt. Let stand for about 30 minutes, then rinse and pat dry. Skin tomatoes and slice thin. Cut bread in cubes and pour melted butter over them.

Butter a souffle dish and put half the zucchini slices in 1 layer in bottom. Season lightly, then lay half the tomatoes over them. Scatter half the basil over tomatoes and sprinkle with sugar. Lay half the cheese slices over tomatoes, then cover with half buttered bread cubes. Repeat the layers, finishing with the bread. Bake for 1 hour at 375 degrees. Serves 4-6.

ZUCCHINI-CARROTS
¼ lb butter
1 pkg herb dressing
1 C grated carrots
1 can cream of celery soup, undiluted
8 oz sour cream
1 TB fresh onion, minced
2 lb zucchini, sliced

Melt butter and mix with herb dressing. Add ½ C grated carrots. Combine soup with sour cream and onions. Add zucchini and remainder of grated carrots. Cover bottom of casserole with half of the dressing mixture. Add zucchini mixture. Top with remaining dressing mixture. Bake 45 minutes at 350 degrees. Serves 6.

ZUCCHINI-CHEDDAR
10 small zucchini (3 lbs)
2 8oz cans tomato sauce
¼ C dried onion flakes
8 oz shredded cheddar cheese

Slice zucchini. Mix with other ingredients in 3 qt casserole. Bake 30 minutes at 350 degrees. Serves 12.

potato latkes

The 20th century latke — do it in your processor

4 large potatoes, unpeeled*
½ small onion
1 egg
1 tsp salt
1 TB flour
¼ tsp baking powder

Process with grating blade. Let grated potatoes stand in a colander about ½ hour. Press down to drain better. Process potatoes and onion using slicing blade. Add other ingredients as batter is being processed.

To fry, use large serving spoon to drop batter into hot oil. Fry both sides until edges turn brown. Drain on paper towels. Serve immediately. May be frozen. To serve when they are frozen, put frozen latkes on a perforated tray or grill over another tray to catch excess oil in 350 degree oven until they are crisp. Serves 6-8.

*Idaho potatoes are best. They are less watery. You don't have to peel them — less work, more vitamins and minerals.

persian vegetable pie

4 TB butter or margarine
1 pkg frozen, chopped spinach, defrosted and
    drained dry
2½ C chopped green onions
1 C chopped lettuce
1½ C chopped parsley
2 TB flour
1½ tsp salt
¼ tsp pepper
½ C chopped walnuts
8 eggs, well beaten
yogurt (optional — do not use with meat meal)

Melt butter in a 9″ x 13″ pan. Combine all the ingredients in a large bowl. Pour into greased pan. Bake at 325 degrees for 1 hour. Spread yogurt on top. Slice into squares. Serve hot or cold.

MOLDS AND SALADS

from tuna to tabbouleh

blueberry salad mold

TOP OF MOLD
1 3 oz pkg lemon jello
1 C hot water
1 8 oz can crushed pineapple
8 oz cream cheese
¾ C cream or half and half
2 TB powdered sugar
1 tsp vanilla

BOTTOM OF MOLD
3 3 oz pkg black cherry jello
4¼ C hot water
1 1-lb can blueberries, drained
1 C blueberry juice

Dissolve the lemon jello with hot water and pineapple juice; the total amount should be 1½ C. Soften the cream cheese gradually with the cream. Add powdered sugar and vanilla. Add small amount of lemon jello to cheese mixture, then gradually all the jello and crushed pineapple. Pour into oiled* 3 qt ring mold and cool. Allow to set.

In the meantime dissolve cherry jello with hot water and blueberry juice; total amount of liquid is 5¼ C. Chill. After jello begins to set, add the blueberries. Carefully pour cherry jello over the lemon jello, which should be almost set. To unmold, use a knife around the edges to loosen onto a platter. Garnish with peach halves, strawberries or grapes.

*You do not have to immerse the ring mold in hot water if you oil it first.

cranberry nut mold

2 3 oz pkg raspberry jello
1½ C hot water
       or
1½ C cranberry juice, heated
1 can cranberries, whole
½ C walnuts, chopped
1 lb can pineapple, crushed
½ C celery, cut up finely

Oil a 4 to 6 C ring mold. Dissolve the jello in hot water or hot cranberry juice and let cool. Add all the ingredients before it jells. Unmold on platter and decorate with peach halves, grapes or strawberries. Double the recipe for a 12 C mold.

frozen cranberry mold

1 1-lb can whole cranberries
1 14oz can crushed pineapple
1 pt non dairy sour cream
1 C chopped pecans

Drain pineapple. Mix with rest of the ingredients. Pour into greased 2 qt ring mold. Freeze. Serve frozen sliced.

This is a pleasant contrast in texture with a turkey dinner, but is not suitable for a buffet if food has to stand a long time.

holiday mold

1 6 oz pkg lemon jello
2 l-lb cans whole cranberry sauce
2 10 oz pkgs frozen strawberries, thawed and drained
1 1-lb can grapefruit sections, drained
1 8¼ oz can pineapple chunks, drained

Combine cranberries and strawberries in saucepan, bring to a boil over low heat, stir in jello until dissolved and well mixed. Add grapefruit and juice. Place in oiled 3 qt mold and refrigerate over night.

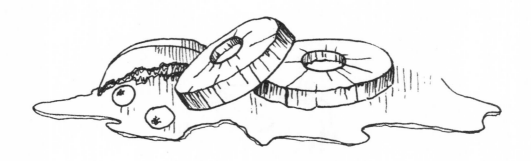

fresh rhubarb mold

3 lb fresh rhubard
2 C sugar
2½ C water
4 envelopes unflavored gelatin
½ C orange juice
2 TB lemon juice

Wash rhubarb. Trim ends. Do not peel. Cut into 1" pieces. Combine rhubarb, sugar, 1¼ C water in a saucepan, bring to a boil, and then simmer until tender (about 10 minutes).

Sprinkle gelatin over remaining 1¼ C water. Stir into hot rhubarb mixture until gelatin is completely dissolved. Add orange and lemon juices. Pour into 10 C ring mold. Chill until firm.

Unmold and fill center with 4 cups strawberries sprinkled with confectioner's sugar, or any seasonal fruit mixture.

taxco salad

Es muy bueno

16 oz red kidney beans
1½ lb ground beef
8 oz french dressing
1 TB chili powder
salt, to taste
3 medium tomatoes, chopped
1 C bell pepper, diced
2 avocados, mashed
½ C mayonnaise
dash hot pepper
¼ C chopped onion
3 C shredded lettuce
tortilla chips

Brown meat in skillet then drain off fat. To meat add kidney beans 2/3 of dressing, chili powder, ½ tsp salt. Cover and simmer 10 minutes. In a separate bowl combine tomatoes, pepper and remaining 1/3 of dressing. Toss well. In a separate bowl, combine mashed avocado, mayonnaise, onion, salt, and hot pepper. Mix well.

To serve, pile on platter in order: tortilla chips, lettuce, meat mixture, tomato mixture, avocado mixture or mix everything together in one bowl (including the tortilla chips) and serve as a one-dish meal.

apple and spinach salad

3 apples, peeled, cored and diced
juice of 2 lemons
3 green onions, sliced thin
3 stalks celery, diced
¼ C mayonnaise
¼ C tahini
2 TB honey
1 bunch spinach, torn into bitesize pieces
¼ C roasted sesame seeds

In a large bowl toss apples, onions and celery. Sprinkle with juice of 1 lemon to keep apples from darkening. In a blender or a small bowl blend mayonnaise, tahina, honey and remaining lemon juice. (Mixture will be very thick) Toss with apple mixture. Cover and chill. Just before serving toss salad with spinach. Serve on a bed of spinach leaves and garnish with sesame seeds. Serves 4 to 6.

greek deli salad

1 green cabbage
2 green peppers
1 red pepper
2 cucumbers, peeled
2 carrots
1 medium onion
2 stalks celery
3 solid (greenish) tomatoes
1 6 oz can Greek olives or pitted California drained
1 12 oz jar herring fillets in wine drained,
    cut in small pieces
¾ C white vinegar
1/3 C water
½ C oil
1 tsp salt or garlic salt
1 tsp white pepper
¼ to ½ C sugar to taste

Slice vegetables fine, using processor if available. Mix all the ingredients and marinate in the refrigerator overnight.

crisp cold vegetable salad

1 large head cauliflower
1 lb fresh green beans
½ C fresh peas
½ lb fresh mushrooms, sliced
3 green onions
1 8 oz bottle Italian salad dressing

Divide cauliflower into flowerettes. Parboil 5 minutes. Rinse with cold water. Cut beans into 1″ pieces. Parboil 5 minutes. Rinse in cold water. Parboil peas 1 minute. Rinse in cold water. Slice onions into small pieces.

Mix all the vegetables overnight in dressing. May be served on individual lettuce leaves. Garnish with chopped hardboiled eggs. Serves 12.

tuned in tuna ring

2 13 oz cans tuna, water packed
8 eggs, hard boiled
2 C celery, chopped
1 bunch green onions, finely cut
¼ C pimiento, cut up
2 C mayonnaise
2 TB lemon juice
½ tsp white pepper
1 C almonds, slivered
parsley, green grapes, olives, cherry tomatoes for garnish

Wash and drain tuna thoroughly. Either by hand, or using food processor, chop tuna, eggs, celery, onion and pimiento. Mix mayonnaise with lemon juice and pepper. Combine tuna, mayonnaise, eggs, vegetables and nuts. Place in a 20 C ring mold, which has been oiled. Chill.

When ready to serve, unmold salad. Fill center with bunches of grapes, cherry tomatoes or black olives. Decorate platter with lettuce leaves.

This salad has served many board meetings. For a smaller mold cut recipe in half and use a 12 C ring mold.

mock mashed potato salad

A low-calorie, filling nutritious vegetable dish

2 10 oz pkgs frozen cauliflower
2 celery stalks
½ green pepper
1 dill pickle
3 TB prepared mustard
2 TB chopped onions
1 tsp salt
½ tsp Worcestershire sauce
½ tsp lemon juice
2 Tb fresh minced parsley

Cook cauliflower according to directions on the package. Drain and mash. Chop celery, pepper, pickle and onion in processor. Blend all ingredients except parsley.

Chill several hours. Sprinkle with parsley and a little paprika. Serve on a bed of lettuce, and decorate with radishes or tomato slices. Serves 6.

salade nicoise

Use your discretion.
Some people don't combine tuna and potatoes.
Some people hate capers or anchovies.
It's up to you!!

½ lb fresh green beans, cooked
1 lb canned tuna, flaked and drained
½ lb sliced new potatoes
3 tomatoes cut in wedges
12 black pitted olives
6 anchovy fillets
1 TB capers, drained
1 large head of lettuce
2 hard boiled eggs, sliced

DRESSING
2/3 C oil (olive preferred)
1 TB lemon juice
2 TB wine vinegar
2 TB Dijon mustard
1 clove garlic, finely minced
1 TB chopped fresh parsley
1 TB fresh basil (if available) or 1 tsp dry
    salt and pepper to taste

Marinate the beans, tuna, warm potatoes, tomatoes. Toss with olives, anchovies and capers. Arrange on lettuce leaves. Garnish with egg slices.

spinach sesame

2 10 oz pkgs frozen spinach, defrosted and drained
    or
1 lb fresh spinach, cooked one minute and drained
¼ C sesame seeds toasted in a dry frying pan
1 TB soy sauce
1 TB water
1 TB sesame oil or peanut or vegetable oil

Combine soy sauce, water and oil. Toss with seeds and spinach. Chill.

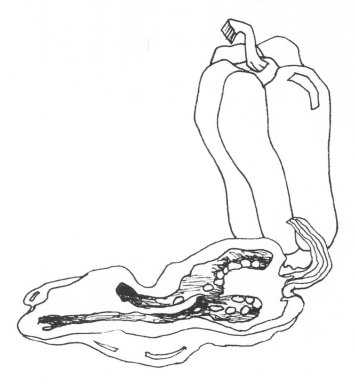

california sweet pepper salad

*The pepper turns red when the farmer decides to
leave the green pepper ripen on the vine*

**5 red and 5 green, or all red or all green peppers,
  cored, seeded, thinly sliced
1¼ C oil
1/3 C red wine vinegar
1 tsp Dijon mustard
¼ tsp salt
¼ tsp pepper
1 red onion, thinly sliced and separated into rings
1 C sliced fresh mushrooms**

In a large skillet, saute peppers in ½ C oil for 10 to 15 minutes, or until limp, stirring often. With a slotted spoon, transfer peppers to a large glass bowl. Drain well and cool for 10 to 15 minutes. If you like your peppers crisp, don't saute them.

Combine remaining oil, vinegar, mustard, salt and pepper and blend well. Add onion rings and mushrooms to the peppers, tossing gently. Pour dressing over pepper mixture and marinate, covered, in refrigerator for 2 to 3 hours. Serve on a lettuce leaf.

tabbouleh

Bulgur Salad

½ C fine cracked wheat (bulgur)
½ C minced green onion
1 C minced parsley
½ C minced fresh mint, optional
2 C coarsely chopped peeled tomatoes
1/3 C lemon juice
½ tsp salt
¼ tsp pepper
1/3 C olive oil
Romaine leaves

Soak wheat in cold water to cover for 10 minutes. Drain and squeeze as dry as possible in clean tea towel or by pressing with back of spoon against sieve. Place drained cracked wheat in a bowl and add green onion, parsley, mint and tomatoes. Stir in lemon juice, salt and pepper. Let stand about 30 minutes to allow flavors to blend. Stir in oil. Pile mixture in bowl and surround with romaine to use for scooping. Makes 6 to 8 servings.

hot fresh fruit salad

3 large navel oranges, peeled and sliced into $\frac{1}{4}''$ slices
1 15½ oz can crushed pineapple, drained
2 large eating apples cored and peeled
8 fresh apricot halves
3 large fresh peaches
1½ C fresh pitted cherries
2 bananas
1 large lemon
5 TB brown sugar
2 TB butter
½ pt sour cream
1 tsp cinnamon

In a 3 qt buttered casserole layer the orange slices. Sprinkle with 1 TB brown sugar. Cover with crushed pineapple. Cover with apples sliced into eighths. Layer with the apricot halves and sprinkle with 1 TB brown sugar. Cover with peaches sliced into eighths. Cover with 1 TB brown sugar. Layer with ¾ C of cherries and then with bananas cut lengthwise. Cover with remaining cherries. Layer with the unpeeled lemon cut into thin slices. Sprinkle with 2 TB brown sugar. Dot the top with the butter.

Heat uncovered in a 350 degree oven for 30 minutes. Combine sour cream and cinnamon and spoon over the top of the individual servings. You may substitute any fruit in season for the above. You may also use canned fruits in combination with the fresh fruits.

pea salad

1 pkg (24 oz frozen peas) thawed on paper towels
6 oz no skin, salted peanuts
1 stalk finely diced celery
2 TB mayonnaise
¼ tsp garlic powder
¼ tsp salt
½ tsp curry powder

Mix all together. May be used to stuff avocado, red pepper or tomato.

zucchini vinaigrette

5-6 medium zucchini
¼ C white vinegar
¼ C white wine or dry sherry
½ C salad oil
1 pkg garlic salad dressing mix
2 TB chopped green pepper
1 TB chopped fresh dill or 1 tsp dried dill
2 TB chopped fresh parsley
¼ C chopped green onions

Trim ends off zucchini. Cut in four to six lengthwise pieces. Cook in boiling salted water for 3 minutes. Drain. Place in serving dish. Combine rest of ingredients and blend thoroughly. Pour over zucchini, turning and coating well. Chill 4 to 6 hours or overnight. Serves 6-8.

refrigerated cole slaw

3 lb cabbage, cut or shredded thinly
2 or 3 medium carrots, grated
2 medium sized onions, finely sliced
¼ C sugar

Mix all together and sprinkle with sugar. Let stand for ½ hour.

Mix together:

1 C white vinegar
1 C white sugar
1 C salad oil
2 TB kosher salt

Bring to a boil and pour over vegetables. When cool place in refrigerator. Can be mixed and spooned into jars and sealed. Will keep up to 3 months in sealed jars.

rainbow pasta salad

East meets West
Chinese salad dressing with homemade pasta

1 lb fettucini*
½ lb fresh broccoli flowerettes
½ lb fresh small button mushrooms
1 red pepper, chopped
¼ C soy sauce
2 TB oil
3 TB oriental sesame oil**
3 TB white wine vinegar
2 garlic cloves, minced
1 tsp sugar

In a large pot of boiling, salted water cook pasta for 3-4 minutes until barely firm to the bite, al dente. Separate with a fork as it cooks. Drain in a colander. Mix with a little oil. Cool. Steam or simmer broccoli in water until barely soft. Plunge immediately into ice cold water to retain green color. Saute mushrooms in oil.

Combine soy sauce, oil, sesame oil, vinegar, garlic and sugar in a jar. Shake to blend well. Toss pasta, vegetables and salad dressing together. Chill. May be made a day ahead. Serves 8-10.

*Fresh, homemade pasta, made daily, is available in many specialty shops. For a rainbow effect use green — made with spinach, red — made with tomato and white.

**Oriental sesame oil is made from *roasted* sesame seeds. This is the key ingredient. There is no substitute for its unique flavor.

tuna salad supreme

1 7 oz can tuna
1 small head lettuce
2 C fresh bean sprouts
4 large fresh mushrooms sliced
½ C diced jicama
1 box cherry tomatoes
1 C cubed cucumber
4 green onions, diced
4½ oz black olives
Add any other vegetables you want

MIX WITH:
1 C mayonnaise
2 tsp soy sauce
2 tsp curry powder

chicken salad

2 C cooked chicken, diced
1 C chopped celery
½ C chopped nuts
¼ C chopped stuffed olives
½ tsp minced onions
½ C mayonnaise
¼ C french dressing

Marinate in refrigerator for 24 hours, or overnight. Can be turned into a mold and served on bibb lettuce, or served from a pretty bowl.

refrigerated cucumber pickles

Go with everything

4 lb cucumbers, cut in ¼″ slices
2 C white vinegar
1/3 C kosher salt
3 C sugar (sugar substitute may be used if desired)
1 lb sliced onions
1 green pepper, chopped
1 4 oz jar pimiento, sliced
1 tsp celery seed

Heat vinegar, salt and sugar until dissolved. Bring to a boil. Cool and pour over vegetables and cucumbers. Refrigerate for 3 days before serving. Mix carefully a few times. Keeps very well for 2 to 3 weeks.

pickled peppers

Are what Peter Piper picked

6 green peppers, whole
1 tsp salt
1 C vinegar
sugar to taste or artificial sweetener
2 cloves garlic
¼ tsp pickling spice
1 C water

Broil peppers until they are sort of black. Keep turning. Remove from oven and put them in a pan and pour salt over them. Omit salt for people on salt free diets. Cover and let stand until cool. Peel peppers. Place in a jar. Mix vinegar with the sugar, garlic and pickling spice. Pour over the peppers and refrigerate. Can be served within a day or two.

salad dressing

1 C safflower oil
¼ C red wine vinegar
1 tsp sugar
1 tsp salt
1 tsp Worchestershire sauce
½ tsp dry mustard
½ tsp paprika
2 cloves garlic, crushed

Blend and refrigerate.

94

kosher style dill pickles

25 to 30 small cucumbers
6 cloves garlic, peeled
3 tsp pickling spice
fresh dill, large sprig for each jar
9½ C water
½ C kosher salt
3 tsp white vinegar

Wash pickles in cold water, dry with paper towels. Place pickles in 3 sterilized qt jars. Put half of the dill in the bottom of the jar and retain the other half to place on the top before closing the jar. Also place 2 cloves of garlic in each jar and 1 tsp pickling spices.

Boil water and salt for a few minutes and add the vinegar. Cool and pour over the pickles. Add the small piece of dill on top. Use new lids and tops and seal the jars tightly. Let pickles sit for 21 days in a cool place. Then keep them in a cool place or in the refrigerator.

black olives

Find somebody with an olive tree. Beg, borrow or steal enough ripe olives to fill 2 qt jars. Prick the olives with the tines of a fork in several places. Put them in a crockpot and cover with cold water for ten days, changing water every four days. This is to get rid of bitterness.

BRINE
10 C water
1 C salt
1 tsp coriander
2 bay leaves
1 tsp fennel seeds
1 orange peel

TO COVER OLIVES IN JARS
olive oil
4 cloves garlic
4 bay leaves

Boil the brine for 15 minutes. Cool and strain over the olives. Leave them in this mixture for 4 or 5 days. Remove olives from mixture and put them in 2 glass jars. Cover each jar of olives with olive oil, 2 cloves garlic, 2 bay leaves and any other spice you desire. Add a little more salt to each jar to taste. Cover tightly and store in a cool place.

garden in a bottle
Make your own sprouts

All you need to raise your own sprouts is a stainless steel screen to fit a mason jar and untreated seeds and grains which can be purchased at your Health Food Store. Alfalfa and mung beans are two of the most popular. You can also sprout rye, wheat, lentils, soybeans, and most any kind of grain or legume.

FOR ALFALFA SPROUTS: For a quart sprout jar use one rounded tablespoon of alfalfa seed. Place seeds in the jar and cover with the strainer top, leaving off the solid lid for storing sprouts in the refrigerator later. Let soak overnight with just enough water to cover, using distilled water or regular water.*

The following morning pour off all the water through strainer top and lay sprout jar on its side. Rinse twice daily under tap through strainer top, by filling about one-third full of water, swish water around, and then pour off all excess water. Shake seeds to side of jar and place on its side. Keep seeds moist but not wet. The strainer top is left on throughout the sprouting process, providing plenty of ventilation. It is not necessary to cover the sprout jar at anytime during the sprouting process.

Continue rinsing morning and evening for about 5 days, at which time, depending on the weather, tiny green leaves will appear. At this point, the more light they are exposed to, the greener and more lush will be the alfalfa sprouts. When the little green leaves are fully open on the alfalfa sprouts they are at the peak of their value and ready to use. Add alfalfa sprouts to salads and sandwiches. They are inexpensive to raise and very nutritious and delicious.

*Do not use artificially softened water

make your own yogurt
A culture for all cultures

Boil milk until it rises in the pan. Cool until you can hold your pinky finger in it to the count of 10 (a quart cools in about a half hour — if it gets too cold, warm it up).

Use one teaspoon of previous yogurt as starter* for each quart of milk you cooked. Put the starter in a bowl and add a little of the warm milk to thin the starter. Then add the rest of the milk and mix well. Put cover on container and wrap it in towels to keep warm. Let stand 3½-4 hours in a warm place until set. Remove lid and shake excess moisture from it. Chill well before stirring.

Tastes best the first week — lasts three weeks or more as starter.

*Or buy dry starter in health food shops

FISH

from cod to coulibiac

salmon, poached in court bouillon

For that special occasion

3-5 lb whole salmon
5 C water
½ C wine vinegar
6 TB sugar
1 TB salt
8 black peppercorns
2 celery tops
2 sprigs parsley
1 bay leaf
fennel seeds or root
1 large onion sliced
1 C white wine

Cook all ingredients except salmon together including fish bones for one hour. Wrap salmon in cheese cloth. Place in court bouillon and simmer for 15 minutes to 1 hour depending on size of fish. Check for flakiness of fish when done. Add juice of ½ lemon and allow to cool in the stock.

Garnish with lemon slices and slices of cold cucumber.

family favorite salmon patties

1 1 lb can salmon
½ C matzo meal or bread crumbs
2 eggs, slightly beaten
3 TB mayonnaise
3 TB ketchup
3 TB butter or margarine

Flake salmon, add crumbs. Combine eggs, mayonnaise and ketchup; stir into salmon. Salt and pepper to taste. Shape into eight patties. Brown in butter. Serves 3 or 4.

salmon with lemon sauce

2 carrots, peeled and sliced
9 small white onions
2 stalks celery
2 TB sugar, or as desired
4 C water
4 slices salmon
1 TB butter
1 TB flour
2 egg yolks
¼ C lemon juice and 2 TB vinegar
salt and pepper to taste

In a skillet or flat pan, place the carrot slices, the peeled onions, sliced celery, sugar and cover with water (approximately 4 cups). Cook for 20 to 30 minutes until vegetables are tender. Then place salmon slices on the vegetables and simmer for about 20 minutes until fish is flaky and soft. Skin and remove bones. Arrange fish on a platter and surround with the vegetables.

Strain fish broth. Make a sauce with the butter and flour, cook for a few minutes. Add the fish broth. Stir and adjust seasonings. Add some of the warm fish broth to the beaten egg yolks and then combine with the sauce. Add more lemon juice and vinegar if necessary. Garnish with lemon slices and parsley. Pass the lemon sauce or pour it over the fish. Can be served warm or cold.

baked fish elegante

1 lb cod fillets
juice of ½ lemon
1 tsp fine herbs
3 TB butter
¼ C fresh parsley
½ C fresh mushrooms, sliced
½ C shredded mozzarella cheese
3 TB milk
dash of paprika

Wash fillets and pat dry. Sprinkle with lemon juice and herbs. Place in well buttered baking pan. Dot with butter. Sprinkle parsley and mushrooms on top. Sprinkle cheese over all.

Put milk on sides of fish being careful not to wash off topping. Shake paprika over all. Refrigerate one hour. Bake in 350 degree oven for 25 minutes.

fish kebabs

1 lb fish (halibut, salmon or sea bass)
¼ cup oil
1 clove garlic
¼ C lemon juice
¼ C beer or wine
¼ C chopped parsley
¼ C soy sauce
salt and pepper
mushrooms, green pepper, pineapple chunks

Rinse fish with cold water. Drain on absorbent paper. Combine oil, garlic, lemon juice, beer, parsley, soy sauce, salt, and pepper to taste in a large bowl. Mix thoroughly and add fish, pineapple, mushrooms, green pepper. Toss to coat ingredients with marinade. Set aside for at least 30 minutes, tossing several times.

Thread long, thin skewers with fish, mushroom, green pepper and pineapple chunks and repeat to fill skewer. Brush kebabs with leftover marinade and place on grill about 4 inches from hot coals. Cook 10 to 12 minutes. Turn kebabs several times while cooking and brush with marinade. May also be broiled. Sprinkle with sesame seeds. Makes 4 to 6 servings.

snappy poached fish

2 lb red snapper fillets
1 1 lb can stewed tomatoes
1 8 oz can tomato sauce
1 small onion, chopped
2 cloves garlic, finely minced
2 TB fresh parsley, chopped
½ C green pepper, chopped
½ tsp sweet basil
juice of 1 lemon
1 TB olive oil
1 tsp salt
¼ tsp white pepper

Rinse and dry fish. Rub with cut side of lemon. Saute onion and garlic in olive oil until soft. Add tomatoes, tomato sauce, parsley, basil, salt and pepper. Cover and simmer 15 minutes. Lay fillets over sauce and baste with sauce. Cover and simmer for 10 minutes. Pour lemon juice over fish, baste again and simmer another 10 minutes. Serves 4.

baked fish mousse

2½ lb whitefish
1 large onion
1 C cream
3 eggs, separated
salt and pepper to taste

Grind fish with onions in food processor. Add cream, egg yolks and seasonings. Fold in beaten egg whites. Put in buttered 6 C mold. Place in a larger pan of hot water. Bake at 350 degrees for 1 hour. Drain off excess juice and reserve for sauce. Cool and refrigerate. May be served hot or cold.

SAUCE
1 C tomato puree
4 TB cream
½ C fish juice from baked mousse

Heat and blend and serve with warm mousse.

Serve cold with sour cream and chopped chives, or add some horseradish and mustard to sour cream, or serve with Green Sauce or Avocado Sauce.

sole with capers

4-5 fillets of sole
3 TB olive oil
1 tsp mustard
3 TB lemon juice
3 TB mayonnaise
3 tsp capers
paprika

Wash fillets and dry thoroughly. Place in a greased pan. Mix oil, mustard, lemon juice, mayonnaise and capers and pour over sole. Sprinkle with paprika. Broil under medium flame until fish is done. (about 10 minutes) Serves 4.

baked fish with tomatoes and rice

(Kammooniyya-Egypt)
Mummy's fish from Egypt

4 firm white fish fillets (to serve 4)
2 large onions, peeled and sliced
3 medium size garlic cloves, peeled and sliced
1 tsp ground cumin
1 C finely chopped celery
½ C canned tomato puree
1 C water (less, if frozen fish fillets are used)
1½ tsp salt
freshly ground black pepper
¼ C vegetable oil, plus 2 TB
1 medium tomato, sliced

Heat ¼ C oil in a heavy skillet, add onions, garlic, cumin. Cook stirring frequently for 7-8 minutes until onions are brown, but do not burn garlic. Remove this mixture to a plate. Add celery to the oil, cook about 5 minutes until soft. Return onions to pan, add tomato puree, water, ½ tsp salt and black pepper. Cook briskly, stirring constantly until liquid has evaporated. Remove from heat.

Wash and thoroughly dry fish fillets. Season with remaining salt. Arrange in an oiled baking pan, side by side. Spread sauce over fish, spreading to the edge of dish. Arrange sliced tomatoes on top and sprinkle with remaining oil. Cover tightly with lid or foil. Bake in preheated 350 degree oven 20 minutes. Remove cover, and bake additional 15 minutes, until sauce is bubbling and tomatoes are lightly browned. Serve with cooked rice.

dill sauce

Great with fish

¾ C mayonnaise
¼ C sour cream
½ C chopped dill pickle
1 tsp celery salt
2 green onions, finely sliced
½ tsp Worcestershire sauce
2 tsp lemon juice
2 tsp dill weed

Mix together the above ingredients and chill for several hours before serving. Yield: 1½ cups.

danish baked fillets

From the land of the midnight sun

6 fish fillets—flounder, halibut or sole, about 2 lb
½ C vegetable broth
juice of ½ lemon
salt
2 TB flour
3 TB butter
1/3 C sour cream, room temperature
2 Tb fresh dill or 1½ tsp dried dill
salt and pepper
minced parsley for garnish

Pat fish dry with paper towels. Place in single layer in baking dish. Cover with broth and lemon juice and sprinkle lightly with salt. Bake covered 10-15 minutes or until fish loses translucency. Transfer fish to platter.

Melt butter in medium skillet. Stir in flour and cook several minutes but do not brown. Remove from heat and gradually add 1 C of liquid from baked fish. Return to heat, stir constantly until thick and smooth. Over low heat, blend in sour cream and dill. Do not boil or sour cream will curdle. If sauce is too thick, add more broth. Season with salt and pepper. Cool. Spoon sauce evenly over fish, covering completely.

Dish may be covered and refrigerated at this point. Remove from refrigerator 2 hours before serving. Just before serving, preheat oven to 400 degrees. Bake, uncovered 10 to 12 minutes or until sauce is bubbly around edges and fish heated through. Sprinkle with parsley and serve immediately.

spinach-stuffed sole

1 pkg frozen spinach souffle (12 oz)
1¾ lb sole fillets (6 pieces)
white pepper and nutmeg, optional
1 can condensed cream of mushroom soup
2 TB dry sherry or lemon juice
1½ C (6oz) swiss cheese, shredded

Let the souffle stand at room temperature for 30 minutes then cut into 6 equal pieces.

Rinse the sole fillets. Pat dry with paper towels. Lightly sprinkle each fillet with pepper and nutmeg. Place 1 portion of souffle on each fillet (or 2 smaller fillets) and wrap the fish around it. Place fish bundles seam side down in a shallow baking dish.

Stir together soup, sherry and a dash each of pepper and nutmeg. Pour mixture over and around fish. Sprinkle cheese on top.

Bake fish uncovered in a 375 degree oven for 30 minutes or until it flakes when prodded with a fork. If desired, lift fish rolls onto a serving platter and spoon sauce around. Makes 6 servings.

fish in eggplant-marinara sauce

4 thick fillets of fish, red snapper or halibut
½ lemon
flour to dredge
salt and pepper to taste
3-4 TB oil
1 1 lb eggplant
1½ TB salt
1 clove garlic
1 green pepper
1 medium onion
8 oz marinara sauce
¼ C vermouth
½ tsp thyme
1 tsp dried basil or 1½ TB fresh basil
¼ C fresh parsley, chopped

Sprinkle juice of ½ lemon over fish. Season with salt and pepper. Dredge with flour. Saute in oil 3 or 4 minutes on each side. Remove from pan and keep warm.

Peel, dice eggplant into ½" cubes, sprinkle with 1½ TB salt. Let sit for 15 minutes. Drain off liquid. Pat dry with paper towel. Saute onion, garlic, green pepper in oil until tender. Add marinara sauce, vermouth, thyme and basil. Simmer covered for 15-20 minutes. Serve over fish. Sprinkle with chopped parsley. Serves 4.

marinara sauce

⅛ tsp thyme
¼ tsp basil
¾ tsp oregano
2 cloves garlic, minced
3 C tomato sauce

green sauce

A colorful accent for fish

1 C mayonnaise
½ C sour cream
1/3 C fresh parsley
½ C fresh spinach
½ tsp dry or 2 tsp fresh dill weed
1½ TB lemon juice

Mix all together in processor until blended smoothly. Chill several hours before serving.

avocado sauce

1 large avocado
4 TB mayonnaise
1 TB tarragon vinegar
2 TB lemon juice
salt and pepper and cayenne to taste

Blend everything smoothly in a processor. Serve with fish mousse.

salmon wellington

Our version of the elegant Russian "coulibiac"

1 pre-rolled frozen sheet of puff pastry 9" x 10"
1½ lb cooked fresh, or canned salmon
2 10 oz frozen chopped spinach
1 C scallions, chopped
½ C fresh parsley, minced
4 TB butter
½ C Madeira wine
½ lb fresh mushrooms, chopped
1 tsp white pepper
¼ tsp each ground cinnamon, ground cloves,
    ground nutmeg
3 hard boiled eggs, sliced
1 raw egg
1 tsp milk

Defrost pastry sheet and roll out to 12" x 16" and ¼" thick. Cook spinach according to directions on package. Drain off all moisture. Saute scallions and parsley in butter until soft. Add mushrooms and spices and simmer for 5 minutes.

Add salmon, gently stir to blend flavors. Cool. Spread half the spinach on dough, leaving 4" margin all around. Top with half the salmon mixture, arrange egg slices and add rest of salmon. Top with rest of spinach.

Fold dough over the filling, sealing top and ends. Roll over onto a cookie sheet. Make small slits in dough to allow steam to escape. Beat egg and milk, and glaze pastry. Bake at 425 degrees for 25 minutes until dough is golden. Serve hot or at room temperature.

italian style fish

1 lb fish fillets (halibut, bass or sole)
1 onion, finely sliced
1 clove garlic
2 TB oil
½ lb fresh or 4 oz can sliced mushrooms
1 8 oz can tomato sauce
½ tsp sugar
½ tsp salt
½ tsp oregano
4 TB parmesan cheese

Saute onion and garlic until tender in oil, add mushrooms, tomato suace, sugar, salt and oregano. Heat for five minutes. Wash fillets and pat dry. Place in a buttered baking dish. Pour sauce over fish. Cover with cheese. Bake in 350 degree oven for 30 minutes uncovered.

fish in wine sauce

2 lb firm fish fillets
enough flour to dredge
4 TB oil
2 cloves garlic, minced
¼ tsp crushed oregano
½ C dry sherry or white wine
5 medium tomatoes, peeled, chopped with juice
            or
1 lb can peeled whole tomatoes with ½ the juice
salt and pepper to taste
2 TB chopped fresh parsley

Wash fish and pat dry. Salt and pepper to taste. Dredge in flour. Saute in hot oil on both sides. Remove fillets to warm platter. Deglaze pan with sherry. Reduce liquid to half. Add tomatoes, juice, oregano and garlic. Simmer one minute to blend. Put fillets back into pan. Simmer until fish flakes easily (about 5 minutes). Serve immediately topped with fresh parsley. Serves 4.

from brisket to b'stila

BEEF, CHICKEN, LAMB AND VEAL

brisket of beef

With flavorful, natural, thick vegetable gravy

5-6 lb brisket
1 1-lb can stewed tomatoes and juice
1 large chopped onion
2 cloves garlic, mashed
5 carrots, cut up
3 stalks celery, cut up
1 tsp Worcestershire sauce
salt and pepper to taste
½ tsp paprika

Place all ingredients except brisket in a heavy roasting pan and simmer on top of the stove about 10 minutes. Place brisket in pan. Roast uncovered at 425 degrees ½ hour. Roast at 325 degrees 1 hour covered. Roast at 325 degrees 1 hour uncovered. Remove brisket and vegetable gravy from pot.

Deglaze pot with a little water by boiling and stirring briskly on top of the stove. Combine deglazed mixture and vegetable gravy and puree in food processor or mash through a food mill or sieve to form a thick gravy. Chill in refrigerator overnight so that you can remove fat. Slice chilled brisket and reheat in defatted gravy. Serves 8.

beef stew

3 lb stew meat, cut in cubes
3 TB oil
2 C beef broth
2 C tomato juice
1 C onion, chopped
1 TB salt
1 tsp oregano
½ tsp pepper
1 bayleaf
2 tsp caraway seeds
8 carrots, sliced
3 potatoes, cubed
1 pkg green beans, sliced frozen
              or
1 pkg peas, frozen

Brown meat in hot oil. Add beef broth, tomato juice, chopped onion, salt, oregano, pepper, bay leaf and caraway seeds. Simmer for one to two hours. Transfer to deep casserole. Add carrots, potatoes and green beans. Bake at 350 degrees until vegetables are tender. If you use peas add them about ten minutes before serving.

short and snappy ribs

3 lb short ribs
½ C brown sugar
2 TB chili powder
1 tsp salt
1 tsp nutmeg
1 tsp celery salt
1 C tomato juice
¼ C vinegar

Sprinkle ribs with seasoned salt. Bake at 350 degrees 1-1½ hours. Drain fat. Mix rest of ingredients. Pour over ribs. Bake another 30 minutes. Ribs may also be barbequed.

jamaican stuffed pumpkin

Peter, Peter pumpkin eater, had a wife and couldn't keep her.
Then they stuffed this pumpkin shell, now they're eating very well.

1 small whole pumpkin, 8-10″ in diameter
2 TB salad oil
2 lb ground chuck
2½ C finely chopped onions
1 green pepper, finely chopped
2½ tsp salt
2 tsp olive oil
2 tsp oregano
1 tsp vinegar
1 tsp ground black pepper
dash of crushed dried red pepper
2 large cloves garlic, mashed
¾ C raisins
1/3 C pimiento-stuffed green olives, chopped
2 tsp capers, drained and minced
1 8-oz can tomato sauce
3 eggs, beaten

Cut a 5″ diameter circular top out of the pumpkin. (Save for lid). Scoop out seeds and scrape pumpkin clean. Place in a large pan, cover with salted water. Bring to a boil, reduce heat, cover and simmer until pumpkin meat is *almost* tender (about 30 minutes). The pumpkin still must hold its shape well. Remove from water, drain and dry the outside. Sprinkle the inside with salt.

Heat salad oil in a frying pan. Add beef, onions and green pepper. Cook over high heat, stirring until meat is brown and crumbly. Remove from heat. Add rest of the ingredients except eggs. Mix well, cover pan and cook 15 minutes, stirring occasionally. Remove from heat. Cool slightly. Mix in the eggs thoroughly. Fill cooked pumpkin with the meat mixture, packing firmly. Place in a shallow greased baking pan and bake at 350 degrees 1 hour. Allow to cool 10-15 minutes before serving.

Carefully lift to a serving plate, garnish with clean leaves. Slice from top to bottom into wedges to serve. Serves 8.

savory steak

By way of Granada, Spain

2 steaks
2 TB margarine
1 tsp rosemary
2 cloves garlic or 1 tsp garlic powder
3-4 oz whiskey
1 tsp oregano
½ lb mushrooms, fresh or canned

Melt margarine in a frying pan, add rosemary and minced garlic cloves. Add steak, pour whiskey over meat, and cook until desired doneness. Remove meat and garlic from pan. Saute oregano and mushrooms for a few minutes. Arrange steaks on a platter, cover with mushrooms. Heat ketchup mixture until warm, pour over steak and serve.

KETCHUP MIXTURE
5 oz ketchup
½ tsp pepper
1 tsp paprika
1 tsp Worcestershire sauce
½ tsp dry mustard

frikadeller

Danish meat balls

1 medium onion, chopped
½ lb veal
½ lb beef
1 egg beaten
1 tsp salt
½ tsp pepper
⅛ tsp nutmeg
½ C bread crumbs
1 C club soda
2 TB oil
2 TB margarine
1 onion, chopped

Grind meat and onion together twice. Add egg, salt, pepper, nutmeg and crumbs. Beat in soda. Shape into oblong balls using 2 tablespoons dipped in water. Heat margarine and oil. Fry onions until brown. Remove from pan. Fry meatballs until browned. Serve with cooked onions on top. Serve with parsley potatoes and red cabbage.

beef borscht

Sauerkraut adds a tangy flavor

2 lb chuck steak (with bone) cut in 2 oz pieces
1 large onion, sliced
2 TB oil
1 lb can whole tomatoes
1 lb can sauerkraut
1 lb can string beets
salt and pepper to taste
¼ C brown sugar, or sugar substitute
1 tsp lemon juice
1 tsp vinegar

Brown meat with sliced onion in oil in a large roasting pan. Add all other ingredients. Bring to a full boil; stir. Cover and simmer about one hour or until meat is done. Meat should become shredded.

holishkes or prakes

It means stuffed cabbage balls

½ C rice
2 lb ground beef
1 tsp salt
1 tsp pepper
1 onion, chopped fine
2 cloves garlic, chopped fine
4 TB brown sugar
6 TB lemon juice
1 large head cabbage
1 can chicken broth
4 TB tomato paste
1 can tomato puree or sauce, 8 oz
½ C white raisins
1 bay leaf
½ tsp cloves
6 gingersnaps, crushed, optional

Parboil rice, add beef, salt, pepper, onion, garlic 1 TB brown sugar and 2 TB lemon juice. Mix all together. Pour boiling water over the cabbage in a large pot. Remove the core of the cabbage and loosen each leaf as it becomes wilted. Let the cabbage cook for about 6 minutes. Pour off the water and continue to separate the leaves. Remove the hard part of the stem of each leaf.

Fill each leaf with 2 TB of the meat mixture and fold over cabbage to roll into a ball. Squeeze gently and leaves will stay together. Fasten each ball with 2 wooden picks. Into a large pot add chicken broth, the rest of the lemon juice, brown sugar, tomato paste, tomato puree, raisins, bay leaf and cloves. Add the cabbage balls.

Simmer for 1½ hours. Adjust seasoning, adding more sugar, salt or pepper as desired. Finish cooking for another half hour until cabbage is soft or place in baking dish in oven and bake at 375 degrees about 45 minutes. Add 6 crushed ginger snaps to sauce when it goes into the oven.

flankenkraut

What ease, what taste, what flavor

3 lb short ribs, flanken or chuck
1 1-lb jar sauerkraut
8 oz tomato sauce
¼ C brown sugar

Mix sauerkraut, tomato sauce and brown sugar and pour over beef. Bake in 325 degree oven for 3 hours, stirring once or twice. Make a day ahead. Skim off fat. Reheat and serve.

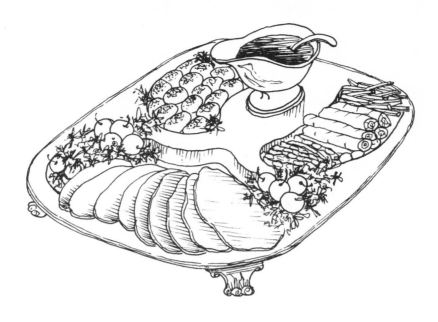

grenadines of beef

the pride of gourmets

8 slices boneless steaks from eye of rib roast ½" thick
¼ C flour
salt, pepper and garlic powder to taste
8 TB margarine
2 large cloves garlic, chopped
½ lb fresh mushrooms, sliced
1 small onion sliced
1 C beef stock
2 tsp soy sauce
½ C dry red wine

Trim all fat from the steaks. Mix flour, salt, pepper and garlic powder in a paper bag. Shake meat slices in the bag. Save the excess flour. Melt 4 TB margarine in a frying pan. Saute the steaks 1½ minutes on each side (for medium rare). Remove from platter. Keep warm.

Melt 4 TB margarine in same pan. Saute garlic, mushrooms and onion. Add stock, soy sauce and wine. Thicken with remaining flour mixture. Cook until thickened. Add the meat. Heat through and serve immediately. If you want the meat well done, cook a little longer in the sauce.

sauerbraten

2 TB oil
3-4 lb beef shoulder clod, rump, brisket or chuck
2 bay leaves
2 large onions, sliced
1 clove garlic
½ tsp salt
½ tsp pepper
¼ C vinegar
¼ C ketchup
2 TB brown sugar, optional
1 C pitted prunes

Heat shortening in skillet, add meat and brown on all sides. Place meat in roasting pan. Add bay leaves, onion, garlic, salt and pepper. Cover and roast at 300 degrees for one hour. Mix vinegar, ketchup and sugar. Pour over the roast and add prunes. Cover and continue roasting until meat is tender, about 2 hours. Serve with potato dumplings, boiled potatoes or potato pancakes. Serves 6.

meatloaf

2 lb ground beef
2 eggs
1/3 C bread crumbs
2/3 C water plus 1/3 cup ketchup mixed together
1 tsp salt
⅛ tsp pepper
⅛ tsp garlic powder
1 TB prepared mustard
1 TB horseradish (red)
1 TB dried minced onion

In a large mixing bowl combine all the ingredients and mix thoroughly. Pack into a loaf pan, 9 x 5 x 3, and bake at 350 degrees for 1 hour.

b'stila

Something special from Morocco, traditionally eaten with the fingers

2 chickens, about 3 lb each
1 C fresh parsley, chopped
1 C fresh coriander*, chopped
1½ C onion, chopped
¼ lb margarine, melted
2 cloves garlic, minced
¼ tsp saffron, optional
1 tsp ground ginger
salt and pepper to taste
4 filo leaves
12 eggs
10 oz blanched almonds, slivered or sliced
1 tsp cinnamon
6 oz granulated sugar
powdered sugar and cinnamon for decoration

Simmer chickens in 4 C water with parsley, ½ C coriander, 1 C onion, garlic, saffron, ginger, salt and pepper. *Do not overcook*. Cool. Bone and cut meat into bite size pieces. Reserve 1 C chicken broth. Remainder makes a great soup stock.

Beat eggs, add 1 C chicken broth, ½ C parsley, ½ C coriander, ½ C onions, 2 tsp salt. Melt 4 TB margarine. Scramble egg mixture until eggs form hard curds. Set aside. Fry blanched almonds in 2 TB oil until golden brown. Cool. Almonds may be ground, chopped or left slivered or sliced. Mix with sugar and cinnamon. Set aside. May all be done ahead up to this point.

Take a 14" round pan (a pizza pan is good). Grease with margarine. Place 2 sheets of filo dough on pan. Layer: ¾ egg mixture, ½ nut mixture, ½ chicken mixture, rest of eggs, rest of chicken and rest of nuts. Cover with 2 sheets of filo, tucking in around sides to make a round package. Brush top with 4 TB melted margarine. Bake in 450 degree oven 30-35 minutes. Sprinkle powdered sugar on top about ¼" thick. With thumb and index finger sprinkle a criss cross design of cinnamon.

*Coriander — also known as cilantro

chicken from mexico

1 roasting chicken
4 TB oil
1 tsp salt
½ tsp freshly ground pepper
3 large onions
3 cloves garlic
1 TB sesame seeds
¼ tsp marjoram
¾ C dry wine
1 C blanched almonds
½ C stuffed olives, sliced
½ tsp chili powder or cumin to taste
2 C chicken broth

Season chicken with salt and pepper. Saute chicken in oil for 15 minutes or until brown. Remove chicken and keep warm. Add onions and garlic to oil remaining in skillet and saute for 10 minutes or until lightly browned. Add sesame seeds, marjoram and wine and simmer for 5 minutes.

Put chicken and wine sauce into a deep casserole. Add almonds, olives and chili powder. Cover and bake in a moderate oven, 350 degrees, for 30 minutes. Uncover and bake 15 minutes more. Serve with rice or noodles.

chicken piccata

1½ lb boned chicken breasts,
    you need 2-3 pieces per person
salt and white pepper to taste
flour to dredge the chicken
2 TB oil
2 TB margarine
1/3 C white wine
2 TB lemon juice
¾ C chicken stock
¼ C fresh chopped parsley
lemon slices for garnish

Flatten breasts until very thin. Season chicken and dredge in flour. Heat oil and margarine together in a frying pan. Brown chicken pieces about 3 minutes on each side. Remove to a warm platter, and keep warm in a 200 degree oven. Deglaze pan with chicken stock. Add wine and lemon juice. Cook until gravy thickens. Add chicken, heat thoroughly. Put on serving platter. Sprinkle with parsley. Garnish with lemon slices and serve immediately.

chicken marsala

Only your butcher knows for sure — veal or fowl play

4 whole chicken breasts, halved and boned
salt and pepper and ground ginger, to taste
flour
2 TB margarine
2 TB oil
1 lb sliced mushrooms
¼ C beef consomme
¼ C marsala wine
¼ C chopped fresh parsley

Pound the chicken breasts flat between two pieces of wax paper. Season with salt, pepper and ginger, and dredge lightly with flour. Melt the margarine and oil together in a frying pan. Saute chicken until golden brown (only a few minutes on each side). Keep warm in 200 degree oven.

Add another TB oil to pan. Saute mushrooms. When soft add consomme and wine. Cook on high heat until sauce is reduced and thickened slightly. Pour over chicken and sprinkle with fresh parsley. Serves 4.

chicken and meatball fricassee

Put it all together it spells MAMA

1 C water
1 lb (about 10) chicken feet, if available*
1 lb chicken giblets and necks
1 tsp salt
¼ tsp ground ginger
¼ tsp pepper
1 small sliced onion
½ C tomato juice
¼ C lemon juice
4 TB brown sugar
2 TB ketchup
1 lb favorite meatball recipe

Simmer first 6 ingredients together ½ hour. Add rest of ingredients and simmer together another ½ hour. Serve in small bowls with challa or rye bread to dip the gravy. Serves 4-6.

*If chicken feet are available they give that good old fashioned flavor and thickness.

one dish baked chicken and rice

2 small chickens, or equivalent favorite parts
½ tsp salt
½ tsp pepper
1 tsp garlic powder
½ tsp ground ginger
1 1-lb can stewed tomatoes
1 tsp salt
2 TB margarine or chicken fat
1½ C rice, uncooked
15 fresh mushrooms
½ green pepper, diced
1 onion, diced

Season chickens with seasoned salt, pepper, garlic powder and ginger. Drain tomatoes. Add enough water to liquid to make 3 cups. Add 1 tsp salt. Grease 9″ x 13″ pyrex dish with margarine or chicken fat. Put in rice, then add mushrooms, tomatoes, peppers and onions. Pour liquid over rice. Place chicken pieces on top, skin side up. Bake in 350 degree oven 1 hour.

chicken puerto vallarta

5 chicken breasts
½-1 C bread crumbs or matzo meal
½ medium onion, minced
1 green pepper, diced
1/3 C oil
2 large limes, sliced
2½ C canned tomatoes (1 lb 4 oz can)
1 tsp salt
1 tsp cumin
2 tsp oregano
1 C raisins steeped in ¼ C sherry
1 6-oz can black olives
salt and pepper to taste

Sprinkle chicken with salt and pepper. Roll in crumbs. Heat oil in skillet and brown. Remove chicken and saute onions and green pepper in same pan until golden. Add tomatoes, raisins, olives and seasonings. Simmer covered for 25 minutes. Line bottom of casserole with slices of lime. Layer sauce, then chicken, then more sauce. Bake covered for 30 minutes at 350 degrees.

green peppercorn sauce
Excellent for duck or steak

2 TB finely chopped shallots
1 clove garlic
3 TB margarine or pan drippings
1 TB concentrated beef stock
salt and white pepper to taste
2 TB green peppercorns, washed and
     drained and mashed
1 TB minced fresh parsley
1 tsp tarragon
¾ C dry sherry or white wine

Saute shallots and garlic in margarine until soft. Add rest of ingredients and simmer until flavors are blended.

polynesian chicken

From the Islands

2-3 lb chicken parts
¼ C brown sugar
½ C soy sauce
1 oz wine vinegar
¼ C pineapple juice
2 green peppers cut in squares
2 white onions cut up
4 stalks celery, diced
1 TB soy sauce
1 tsp sugar
3 TB water
1 tsp cornstarch
1 bunch scallions
8 oz can pineapple chunks

Brown chicken pieces in oil in a skillet. Transfer to a baking pan. Mix brown sugar, soy sauce, vinegar and pineapple juice together and pour over chicken. Bake 30 minutes covered at 325 degrees. Remove cover and bake 30 minutes at 400 degrees.

Meanwhile, saute onions in oil until tender. Add peppers and celery and scallions and saute 3 minutes. Mix soy sauce, sugar and water and cornstarch. Add to vegetable mixture and cook one more minute. When chicken is done, pour vegetable mixture over it. Add pineapple chunks. Heat through. Serve with rice. Serves 6.

chicken marengo

3 lb fryer, cut up (or all boneless breasts for party)
¼ C flour
1 package spaghetti sauce mix
¾ C dry red wine
12 cherry tomatoes
12 tiny white onions, peeled by dropping in boiling water
    for 10 seconds, then in cold water. Skins will slip off.
12 medium mushrooms, cleaned whole

Coat chicken with flour. Place skin side up in baking dish. Combine spaghetti sauce with wine. Pour over chicken. Bake for one hour at 350 degrees. Add vegetables and bake 15 minutes longer. Serve over rice.

baked chicken stuffed with vegetables

1 3-lb whole chicken, or chicken quarters
1 C white wine or apple juice for basting

Split whole chicken entire length of back, removing backbone from tail to neck. Open it out, skin side up. With mallet or cleaver flatten with a firm whack, fracturing breast-bone and ribcage. Turn over and take out ribcage and cartilage with a very sharp boning knife taking care not to break the skin.

4 TB oil
½ tsp each basil and thyme
3 thinly sliced onions

Line a broiler pan with the onions. Rub the chicken with the oil and herbs. Marinade for at least 2 hours.

STUFFING
5 zucchini, shredded
1 carrot shredded
1 onion, finely chopped
1 large clove garlic, minced
3 TB margarine
½ tsp marjoram
1 egg
2 TB bread crumbs (or use matzo meal for Passover)
salt, pepper and nutmeg to taste

In a large bowl, layer shredded zucchini, sprinkling them with salt and set aside for 30 minutes. Squeeze liquid out with hands or towel and fluff up. Saute carrot, onion and garlic in margarine until soft. Add zucchini and additional margarine if needed and mix with a wooden spoon to avoid sticking. Add marjoram, egg, breadcrumbs and seasonings. Saute until dried and has a stiff consistency. Cool.

Working with the fingertips, separate skin from meat of chicken, being careful not to tear skin. Stuff with vegetables stuffing, forcing it into place, and mold the skin. Fill drumsticks and thighs first. Place in broiler pan over onions. Bake in a 450 degree oven for 10 minutes. Reduce temperature to 375 degrees and bake for 1 hour longer. Baste every 20 minutes with wine or apple juice. If chicken browns too quickly, cover loosely with foil. Remove foil the last 10 minutes for crispness. Serves 4.

fruited cornish hen

4 cornish hens (20 oz each)
2 tsp paprika
1 tsp garlic powder
4 TB oil
2 tsp salt
3 apples peeled, cored and cubed
8 pitted prunes
4 apricots
4 TB apricot jam plus 1 TB orange juice (for glaze)
4 tsp apricot jam

In a small bowl combine the paprika, garlic powder, oil and salt. Rub the birds with this mixture several hours before the birds are to be baked. Combine the fruit with apricot jam. Fill the birds with the fruit mixture. Bake on rack uncovered at 350 degrees for 45 minutes. Spread glaze on birds and bake for 15 minutes more.

gefilte chicken
No it's not fish, it's chicken

2 whole chicken breasts, skinned and boned
2 eggs beaten
2 TB matzo meal
2 onions sliced
1 tsp salt
½ tsp pepper
1 large onion sliced
2 TB chicken fat or margarine
1 C chicken stock

Steam 2 sliced onions in about 2-3 TB of water for 10 minutes or until soft. Cool. Chop (or use processor) chicken, cooked onion, salt, pepper, eggs and matzo meal together. Saute 1 large onion sliced in chicken fat until golden brown. Put in pot with 1 C stock and let come to a boil. Drop chicken mixture by rounded tablespoon into stock, lower heat, cover and simmer for ½ hour. May be served hot or cold.

chicken in caper sauce
A fowl caper

4 lb chicken parts or boned breasts
2 TB flour
salt and pepper to taste
6 TB margarine
1½ C dry white wine
4 TB capers, drained
4 TB lemon juice
1 package frozen artichoke hearts, thawed
18 whole peeled white onions
18 cherry tomatoes

Wash chicken parts and pat dry. Season with salt and pepper and dredge with flour. Melt margarine in heavy pan. Brown chicken parts. Remove from pan. Deglaze pan with wine.

Add capers, lemon juice, artichoke hearts, onions and chicken. Cook ½ hour covered turning chicken a few times. Add tomatoes and cook 15 minutes longer. Serve with cooked rice. Serves 6-8.

glaze for broiled or barbequed chicken

A shiny flavorful glaze

Combine:

> ¼ C french type prepared mustard
> ¼ C corn syrup (light)
> ¼ C minced green onion
> ½ tsp basil
> ½ tsp tarragon
> pinch of thyme

This is enough for 2 quartered fryers. About 10 minutes before chicken is done, brush with the mixture, turning once.

vegetable and bread stuffing

> 10 C fresh bread crumbs (about 28 slices)
> ¾ lb fresh mushrooms, sliced
> 2 TB margarine
> 2 onions, shredded
> 6 medium carrots, shredded
> 6 stalks celery, shredded
> 4 TB margarine
> 6 eggs
> 1 can chicken broth, full strength
> ¼ lb margarine, melted
> ½ tsp white pepper
> 1 tsp dill weed
> 1 tsp tarragon

Prepare the bread crumbs in the food processor, or crumble lightly with your fingers, but do not crush. In a large frying pan, saute mushrooms in 2 TB margarine. Remove from pan. Add the onions, carrots and celery and 4 TB margarine. Cover and let steam until tender. Add the mushrooms.

Beat the eggs lightly and mix with bread crumbs. Add all the vegetables. Add the chicken broth, melted margarine, pepper, dill and tarragon. Bake in a 9″ x 13″ casserole for one hour at 350 degrees. Cover for ½ hour and then bake uncovered so the dressing will brown and have a nice crust. Serves 12 or stuffs a 24 lb turkey.

(½ C stuffing for each pound of turkey)

oven coq au vin

2 fryers cut up, or chicken parts of your choice
¼ C flour
1 TB seasoned salt
4 TB margarine
1 can beef broth, undiluted
½ C dry sherry

Lightly coat chicken parts in flour mixed with seasoned salt. Fry in a skillet with margarine until browned. Place in a baking dish and pour broth and sherry over chicken.

The chicken can be prepared ahead up to this point and refrigerated. Bake in a 350 degree oven for 1-1½ hours, basting very often. Cover with foil when it becomes well browned so that the chicken will stay moist.

viva mama's spaghetti sauce

¼ C olive oil
2 medium sized onions, chopped
1 lb meat balls, seasoned
1 lb ground beef
1-2½ lb can tomatoes
2 cans tomato paste
1½ C water
1 tsp salt
1 tsp chili powder
6 cloves garlic
fresh basil, optional
mushrooms, optional

Heat oil in skillet. Saute onions until barely browned and then lift them out carefully into large kettle. Brown meatballs in oil left in skillet. When well browned, put in kettle with onions. Brown remaining meat, stirring constantly to prevent lumping. Turn this also into kettle. Add remaining ingredients. Pierce garlic cloves with fork. Cover and simmer 1½ hours. Remove garlic.

Yields 7 cups sauce.

lamb chardash

With a Hungarian flavor

4 round bone lamb chops
2 TB vinegar
1 large onion, grated
2 TB vegetable shortening
salt and pepper to taste
3 cloves garlic, crushed
2 TB paprika
1 8-oz can tomato sauce
1 C water
3 stalks celery
1 large green pepper, diced
1 tart apple, grated
1 4-oz can large button mushrooms or ½ lb fresh

Trim all fat from lamb chops. Soak in vinegar for ten minutes, then wash thoroughly in cold water before sauteing. In a roasting pan brown onions in shortening, add garlic, salt and pepper to taste, and paprika.

Dry lamb chops thoroughly. Saute chops in browned onions on low heat until brown. Add tomato sauce and 8 oz water to cover chops. Simmer for one hour. Add celery, green pepper, grated apple and mushrooms. Continue simmering on low heat. If more water is needed, add a little. Watch it carefully. Should be ready in one more hour. Serve with rice or kasha. Serves 4.

lamb marinade

1 C orange juice
1 tsp pepper
1 TB seasoned salt
1 tsp mustard
juice of ½ lemon

mimi had a little lamb

6 lamb shanks
¾ C gin
½ C oil
½ C wine vinegar
1 onion chopped
1 clove garlic, minced
1 tsp tarragon
1 tsp basil
2 tsp salt
2 tsp ground pepper
1 TB cornstarch

Combine all ingredients except the cornstarch and marinate lamb all day or refrigerate overnight. Arrange shanks in a shallow pan and bake two hours at 350 degrees, basting often with marinade. Remove meat to platter. Skim fat from pan juices. Pour juices into a two cup measure, add cornstarch which has been softened in ½ C cold water. Return to pan and cook until thickened. Pour hot sauce over meat and serve with rice or barley pilaf.

sikbaj
Stew from North Africa

1½ lb lamb or beef cut into 2″ cubes
2 TB olive oil
1½ C beef consomme
1 tsp cinnamon
1 C peeled and sliced carrots
1½ C onions, chopped
2 tsp lemon juice
1 TB coarsely ground pepper
2 TB wine vinegar
½ C honey
½ lb figs, fresh or canned, drained (reserve juice)
1 C sliced almonds
½ C raisins (soaked in juice from figs)
½ C fresh parsley, chopped

Brown meat cubes in hot oil in roasting pan. Add consomme, cinnamon, carrots and onions. Cover and simmer 1½ hours. Add lemon juice, pepper, vinegar and honey. Cook another hour, stirring occasionally. Add figs, almonds and raisins and cook 5 minutes longer. Sprinkle with parsley. Excellent served with rice, spinach, salad and fresh fruit. Serves 6.

potted lamb
Without that lamby flavor

2 lb boned lamb shoulder (fat completely removed)
2 TB oil
¼ C minced onion
2 or 3 minced cloves garlic
salt and pepper to taste
2 C boiling water
1 beef bouillon cube
2 tsp celery seeds (not celery salt)
2 tsp Worcestershire sauce
2 TB snipped fresh parsley

Remove excess fat, skin and gristle. Cut lamb into 2″ cubes or smaller. In hot oil, in a roasting pan, saute minced onion and garlic until golden and tender. Remove from pan and set aside. In hot oil left in pan brown lamb well on all sides. If liquid appears while browning, allow to accumulate for about ten minutes of cooking time.

Dissolve bouillon cube in boiling water. Add salt, pepper, browned onion and garlic, dissolved bouillon, celery seeds and Worcestershire sauce. Simmer gently, covered, one and a half hours. Remove excess fat on surface. With cover off, allow liquid to boil down to consistency of thin gravy. This clings to lamb with enough extra to spoon over rice or noodles. Sprinkle with fresh parsley.

dilled veal stew

2 lb lean veal, cut in 1" cubes
¼ C flour
¼ C margarine or oil
2 onions, sliced
2 cloves minced garlic
½ lb carrots, sliced
1 turnip sliced
1 rutabaga sliced
1 C chopped tomatoes
¼ C dry sherry
1 C chicken stock
1 tsp seasoned salt
¾ tsp basil
½ tsp thyme
1 bay leaf
2 TB fresh chopped dill
freshly ground pepper

Mix seasoned salt with flour. Dredge veal cubes. Shake off excess flour. Heat oil in roasting pan. Brown meat, then onions, garlic and vegetables. Lift out meat and vegetables, add sherry and stock. Scrape bottom of pan with spoon (deglaze). Add seasonings and return meat and vegetables to pan. Cover and bake at 350 degrees for 1½ hours. Serve over rice or noodles. Serves 6.

veal shanks italiano (osso buco)

4 lb veal shanks
salt and pepper, to taste
flour, enough to dredge
3 TB margarine
3 TB oil
2 onions, diced
2 cloves garlic, minced
1 C beef stock
3 oz tomato paste
1 C white wine
½ tsp each thyme, basil and oregano

Season veal with salt and pepper. Dredge with flour. Heat margarine and oil together in a heavy pan. Saute veal shanks until browned. Saute onions and garlic until limp. Remove from pan. Deglaze pan by adding beef stock and scraping the pan. Add tomato paste, wine and herbs. Bring to a boil. Lower heat. Add veal and onions and garlic. Simmer covered about 1 hour. This dish is even better made a day ahead and reheated. May be frozen. Serve over rice, linguine or green noodles. Serves 6.

132

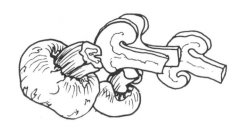

veal stew with onions and mushrooms

3-4 lb veal stew, cut in 2″ pieces
1-2 lb veal bones (optional)
2½ C chicken broth
1 large onion, stuck with 1 whole clove
1 large carrot
1 stalk celery
herb bouquet (4 parsley sprigs, ½ bay leaf, ½ tsp
    thyme tied in cheesecloth bag or a metal teaball)
salt to taste
18-24 white pearl onions
1 TB margarine
½ lb fresh mushrooms, sliced or button
2 tsp lemon juice
4 TB margarine
5 TB flour
salt, white pepper to taste

Place veal and bones in large pot. Cover with cold water and bring rapidly to simmer. Simmer for 2-3 minutes until scum finishes rising. Drain through colander into sink. Wash out pot. Rinse veal, return to pot.

Add chicken broth, vegetables and herbs, and enough cold water to cover. Simmer slowly, partially covered 45 minutes to 1 hour. Do not overcook. Meat should be tender but not too soft. Discard bones and vegetables. Keep veal in broth so it will not discolor and keep warm. Peel onions by dropping into a large pot of boiling water. Bring back to a boil and boil for 30 seconds. Drain and peel. Arrange in one layer in frying pan, add ½ C veal cooking liquid, ½ tsp salt and 1 TB margarine. Cover and simmer slowly for 15 minutes until onions are tender when pierced with a knife.

To make sauce, melt 4 TB margarine, stir in 5 TB flour, cook slowly until mixture bubbles but does not turn brown. Remove from heat. Vigorously beat in a ladleful of veal liquid. Reset on stove and keep adding more liquid slowly to make a smooth gravy. Liquid from cooked onions may also be used. You should have about 3 C of gravy. Add mushrooms. Simmer about 10 minutes. Adjust the taste with salt, pepper and lemon juice. Add veal. Mix thoroughly and serve with noodles or rice. Serves 8.

stuffed pocket of veal

1 5-lb breast of veal
½ tsp each salt and white pepper, sprinkled in pocket
6 onion rolls, Kaiser, dried out in oven and grated
4 onion rolls, soaked in hot water, then squeezed out
½ lb mushrooms, fresh
4 TB margarine, for sauteing vegetables
4 carrots, shredded
4 stalks celery, shredded
1 onion, thinly sliced
5 eggs
4 TB margarine for bread mixture, melted
½ tsp dill weed
½ tsp tarragon
1 can chicken broth
salt and white pepper to taste

Have butcher prepare veal pocket. Dust inside of pocket with salt and pepper. Prepare bread dressing as follows: Grate the dried out onion rolls by hand or with food processor. Combine with the wet onion rolls. Set aside. Saute carrots, celery and onion in 3 TB margarine. Cover and steam until tender. Saute mushrooms in separate pan with 1 TB margarine. Add to vegetables. Beat eggs slightly and mix with bread crumbs. Combine with all the vegetables, add 4 TB melted margarine, dill weed, tarragon and chicken broth. Add salt and pepper to taste.

Stuff dressing into veal pocket. If there is too much dressing, bake some in a covered casserole. Use skewers or thread and needle to secure pocket. Bake in a covered roasting pan at 325 degrees for three hours. Uncover for one-half hour to brown. Slice and arrange on a serving platter.

perfect for Pesach

ENTREES AND DESSERTS FOR PASSOVER

ISRAELI

2 apples, peeled and chopped
3 bananas, mashed
½ C peanuts, chopped
½ orange, juice and rind
½ lemon, juice and rind
¼ C sweet red wine
2 tsp cinnamon
sugar to taste

Blend everything together.

ASHKENAZI

2 C apples, peeled and chopped
1 C walnuts or pecans, chopped
¼ C sweet red wine
3 TB honey
2 tsp cinnamon

Finely chop apples and nuts together. Blend together with all other ingredients.

SEPHARDIC

½ C sliced dates, pitted
½ C dried apricots
2 C apples, peeled and chopped
½ C walnuts, chopped
1 TB sweet red wine
1 TB sugar

Combine dates, apricots and apples. Add water to cover. Cook on low heat until tender enough to mash, at least ½ hour. Drain water. Mash. Add nuts, red wine and sugar. Blend together.

YEMENITES season chopped dates, figs, sesame seeds with hot chili pepper.

ITALIANS add chopped hard boiled eggs to the Ashkenazi mixture.

hadassah haroset

*The tradition is the same — its supposed to resemble mortar
used by us when we were slaves in Egypt —
but the variations are infinite*

passover meat loaf

1 large onion
2 lb hamburger
2 garlic cloves, peeled and pressed
12 eggs, beaten
3 matzos
salt and pepper to taste

Break matzo into small pieces. Moisten in hot water and squeeze out all moisture. Saute onion in oil. Brown beef. Mix everything together and bake in greased 13" x 9" pyrex pan at 350 degrees 45 minutes to 1 hour.

passover meat pie

To soften the heart of the Pharaoh

FILLING
1¾ lb ground cooked beef (brisket or stew)
1 stalk celery
2 onions, chopped
2 beaten eggs
seasonings to taste
chicken fat

Saute celery and onions in "lots" of chicken fat. Add meat and eggs. Mix thoroughly.

CRUST
1 lb matzo farfel, dampened with water
3 TB powdered chicken soup concentrate
4 beaten eggs
1 TB chicken fat
1 tsp garlic powder
½ tsp pepper

Mix all together thoroughly. Grease 8½" x 13" pan with chicken fat. Line bottom with ½ of the crust. Put in filling. Top with remainder of crust. Bake in 350 degrees oven about 1 hour.

matzo dumplings

6 matzos
3 TB chicken fat or margarine
1 large onion, chopped
3 TB chopped fresh parsley
3 large eggs
1½ tsp salt
½ tsp nutmeg
¼ tsp ginger
¼ tsp pepper
1-2 TB matzo meal

Soak matzo in water. Squeeze dry with your hands. Put in colander over a bowl, press down with a weighted plate, cover and let stand overnight. Heat fat in large skillet, add onions, fry until golden brown. Add parsley, mix well. Add matzos and stir until completely mixed. Remove from heat. Add slightly beaten eggs and seasonings and matzo meal. Refrigerate for 2 hours.

Shape into 2-3 inch balls, adding matzo meal if they are too soft. Drop into a large pot of boiling salted water and simmer uncovered about 15 minutes, until they float. Remove with slotted spoon. Serve with brisket or stew with lots of gravy or place in oven with roasting chicken for the last 20 minutes of roasting. Makes about 10 dumplings.

fruit kugel

8 matzos
8 eggs
1 tsp salt
½ C sugar
1 16oz can crushed pineapple
2 large pippin apples, chopped
1 C raisins plumped in apple juice
¼ lb margarine, melted

Break up and soak matzos in boiling water for 2-3 minutes. Pour off excess water, but the mixture should not be too dry. Beat eggs, salt and sugar. Add matzo, pineapple, apples and raisins. Add melted margarine. Pour into well greased 9″ x 13″ pan and spread evenly. Bake in 350 degree oven for 1 hour.

passover wine and nut cake

12 egg whites (should be 1 2/3 C)
1½ C sugar
12 egg yolks, beaten
8 TB sweet wine or Israeli brandy or Slivovitz*
1 lemon, rind and juice, ¼ C
1 orange, rind and juice, ¼ C
1½ C cake meal
1 TB potato starch
½ tsp cinnamon
1½ C walnuts or pecans, chopped

Beat egg whites until stiff, add sugar gradually. Beat egg yolks well and add the wine and/or brandy and citrus juices. Add the cake meal, potato starch and cinnamon. With a folding motion using a wire whisk, carefully combine the two egg mixtures. Add the nuts last. Prepare an angel food cake pan by wetting it and sprinkling cake meal around the pan. Shake off the excess. Cake pan will be quite full. Bake at 350 degrees for about 1 hour. Test for doneness with a wooden pick. Invert pan until cake cools. Use a knife to loosen edges of the cake and the center stem. Invert pan over cake tray and wait for it to come down. Can be frosted or dusted with powdered sugar, or it is just as good served plain.

*After Passover use 8 TB Grand Marnier, Benedictine or Triple Sec, or some of each. This cake is moist and can pass for a good nut cake any time of the year.

potato torte

2 large baking potatoes
7 eggs separated
1 C sugar
grated rind of 1 lemon
1 TB lemon juice
½ C ground almonds

Boil potatoes in their skins *at least 2-3 days ahead*. Dry out (outside refrigerator). Peel and grate coarsely to make 3 C. Cream egg yolks with sugar until light yellow in color and double in bulk.

Add lemon rind, juice and almonds. Mix well. Stir in potatoes. Again mix well. Fold in beaten egg whites. Pour into greased 10″ spring form that has been sprinkled with matzo meal. Bake at 375 degrees for 1 hour or until toothpick comes out clean.

matzo kugelettes

*Ma nishtana . . . why is this muffin different from all others . . .
because its a kugelette*

3 matzos or 1½ C matzo farfel
3-4 tart apples, peeled and shredded
½ C raisins, plumped in apple juice for a few hours
1/3 C brown sugar
½ tsp cinnamon
½ tsp salt
6 eggs, beaten
¼ C melted margarine
½ C blanched almonds, chopped (2½ oz)
1 orange rind, grated

Break up matzos. Pour boiling water over and toss. Squeeze out all water. Cool. Add all the ingredients, eggs last and spoon in greased muffin tins, ¾ full. Bake 25-30 minutes at 350 degrees until nicely browned. Serve warm. Makes 18 muffins.

Can be made earlier and reheated. Can be frozen. Double this recipe fills a 13″ x 9″ pyrex baking dish. Bake about 45 minutes.

matzo farfel kugel

Starts out like a wet glob, but watch it puff up in the oven into a light, fluffy creation

4 eggs
2½ C farfel
2¼ C water
pinch pepper
1 TB salt
½ tsp onion salt
½ C chicken fat or margarine

Warm eggs in the shell, in hot tap water and set aside. Mix farfel, water, pepper, salt and onion salt. Melt fat, mix with farfel and let set. Beat eggs with ¼ C water until fluffy. Add to farfel mixture. Put mixture in a well-greased 1½ qt pyrex baking dish. Bake for 30 minutes at 350 degrees. Turn the whole mixture over to make bottom crusty. Bake 30 minutes longer.

passover mocha nut cake

8 eggs separated
¼ tsp salt
1 TB lemon juice
1½ C sugar
¾ C matzo cake meal
¼ C potato starch
½ C strong coffee
½ C finely chopped walnuts

Beat whites. Add salt, lemon juice. Continue beating adding ½ C sugar slowly. Beat until stiff. Beat yolks with sugar until light. Add to white mixture. Sift cake meal and starch. Fold into mixture, alternating with coffee. Fold nuts in carefully. Bake in ungreased 9″ tube pan at 325 degrees for 50 minutes. Raise to 350 degrees and bake for 10 minutes more. Invert pan and cool completely.

Use Chocolate Torte Glaze or Cassata Cake Chocolate Frosting.

chocolate torte

Don't wait for Passover to serve this

6 oz semi-sweet chocolate
10 eggs separated at room temperature
1 C sugar
2 C finely chopped walnuts

Melt chocolate in double boiler. Cool. Beat egg yolks with sugar until very thick and lemon colored. Stir in the chocolate. Add the nuts. Beat egg whites until stiff but not dry. Fold into the chocolate mixture. Grease a 9" spring form pan and line bottom with wax paper. Turn mixture into pan and bake at 350 degrees 1 hour.

CHOCOLATE GLAZE
8 oz semisweet chocolate
1 TB oil
4 TB butter or margarine

Melt chocolate in double boiler. Add oil and butter a small piece at a time to dissolve thoroughly. Spread over cake.

passover chocolate nut torte

8 eggs, separated
¾ C sugar
2½ C finely ground walnuts (almonds make cake lighter)
2½ TB chocolate syrup or 2 oz semi-sweet
    chcolate melted

CHOCOLATE GLAZE
4 oz semi-sweet chocolate
¼-½ C strong coffee
1 tsp butter

Beat egg yolks and sugar until lemon colored and triple in volume. Add nuts and chocolate syrup. Fold in stiffly beaten egg whites. Bake in 9″ spring form, of which bottom *not sides* has been greased. Bake at 350 degrees for 45 minutes, or until a toothpick comes out clean. Cool in the pan. Glaze.

To make glaze, melt chocolate in double boiler and add coffee and butter. Stir until smooth.

passover almond cookies

1 C matzo farfel
1 C sugar
1 TB matzo cake meal
pinch of salt
¼ lb butter or margarine, melted
1 egg, beaten
½ tsp vanilla
½ C finely ground almonds

Crumble farfel into very small pieces. Mix with sugar, cake meal and salt. Blend in melted butter. Add egg and vanilla, mixing well. Mix in almonds. Put ungreased foil on a baking sheet. Drop cookie mixture, by teaspoon about 2″ apart. Cookies will spread. Bake at 325 degrees, 8-10 minutes, until edges turn brown. Cool. Peel off foil. Makes 5 dozen cookies.

passover chocolate chip sponge cake

   9 eggs, separated
   1½ C sugar
   ½ C potato starch
   ¼ C matzo cake meal
   ¼ tsp salt
   6 oz semi-sweet chocolate, grated

Beat whites until stiff. Add half of the sugar gradually. In another bowl beat yolks until very thick and creamy. Add rest of the sugar to beaten yolks.

Sift together potato starch, cake meal and salt. Gently add sifted ingredients and grated chocolate to yolk mixture. Gently fold into egg white mixture. Bake in an ungreased tube pan at 325 degrees for 1 hour. Invert pan to cool.

Use a chocolate glaze for top or serve with whipped cream and sliced strawberries.

from frying pan to wok

CHINESE, JAPANESE AND KOREAN

Discover the joy of *oriental cooking*. A few pages barely do justice to a sophisticated cuisine of wide range. There are many styles which have been developed over thousands of years, but don't be timid, our recipes are easy and varied and designed to encourage you to add drama and variety to your repertoire. Although it is more a matter of different techniques than exotic ingredients, you will find that most supermarkets now have an oriental food section. The Chinese hardly ever use dairy products so it is easy to plan a kosher meal.

Bean Curd (tofu) or soybean cake is a low-fat, high protein favorite of vegetarians. Its own flavor is bland, but it absorbs the flavor of other foods. Available in supermarkets or health food stores. Store in refrigerator. Before using, rinse and drain in cold water. Will keep for one week.

Bean Sauce* is a thick, salty sauce made from fermented soy beans, salt, flour and sugar.

Bean Threads (sai fun) or vermicelli are translucent, cellophane noodles made from mung bean flour. Soften 30 minutes in warm water and use in soups and stir-fried dishes.

Bok Choy is Chinese cabbage. All parts are edible, sweet and mild.

Chili oil, paste or dried chile peppers are used in hot Szechwan dishes. Enjoy sparingly at your own risk.

Fresh Ginger Root is indispensable in oriental cooking. It may be stored dry at room temperature for 10 days. When frozen the texture changes but not the flavor. Mince and keep in sherry in a tightly covered jar in the refrigerator indefinitely.

Hoisin Sauce* is made from soybeans, flour, sugar, vinegar and spices. It is especially good with duck.

148

Oil* may be strained and used over again many times. Fry some green onion and ginger root in it for 5 minutes to remove the flavor of previous cooking. Any light peanut, corn or polyunsaturated oil may be used. Do not use sesame or safflower oil for stir-frying.

Plum Sauce or duck sauce is made from plums, chiles, sugar, vinegar and spices.

Rice, short or medium grain is used because the sticky little clumps can easily be handled with chopsticks. Also use it for your molded rice rings. Long grain produces fluffy, separate grains.

Rice Sticks *(mai fun)* are opaque, dried, thin noodles made of ground rice. They puff up in seconds when deep fried, or may be briefly soaked in water and used in soup or noodles dishes.

Sesame Seed Oil* is made from roasted sesame seeds. It is dark, aromatic and used sparingly as a distinctive seasoning.

Soy Sauce is made of soy beans, wheat flour, salt, yeast and water. Saltiness and density vary with each brand. May be kept on your shelf indefinitely.

Stir-Frying means cooking and stirring vigorously in a small amount of oil over high heat for a few minutes. Vegetables retain their fresh color, and thin slices of chicken or beef quickly absorb seasonings and remain juicy and tender.

Wok is the Chinese all purpose bowl-shaped cooking pan. A well seasoned wok has been coated with oil and heated several times. It is cleaned only with hot water and gets black with age.

*Can be refrigerated several months after opening.

the art of won ton

It's so easy when you can buy prepared "skins"

FILLING
enough for about 60 won ton "skins" or 1 package
1 lb ground veal
1 TB sherry
2 TB soy sauce
½ tsp garlic salt
4 water chestnuts minced fine
3 green onions, minced fine
½ tsp sugar
1 egg

Combine all ingredients.* Remove skins from package. Cover with a damp towel so they won't dry out. Put 1 tsp filling in the center of each skin. The floured side should be on the outside. Gently press edges together by folding in half. Seal with a little water. They are ready to be deep fried for appetizers or used in soup.

*If you like a soft, light filling, stir fry before putting it in the skins.

chicken soup variations

Add an oriental flavor to our Jewish classic

Bring 6-8 C chicken broth to a boil. To thicken: blend 1 TB cornstarch with 2 TB water. Boil until thick and clear. To enhance the flavor add 1 TB sherry or a few drops of oriental sesame oil. For egg drop soup: Scramble an egg. Drop into boiling soup and serve immediately.

Add any combination of the following: sliced mushrooms, sliced water chestnuts, fresh spinach leaves, shredded bok choy, chinese pea pods, cut up green onions or pieces of fresh bean curd.

DEEP FRIED WON TON APPETIZERS

Prepare won tons as directed. Heat 2 C oil in wok. Test with a piece of won ton skin to see if it sizzles. Deep fry a few won tons at a time until golden brown. Drain on a paper towel. Keep warm to serve with sauce.

SWEET AND SOUR SAUCE
4 TB ketchup
4 TB sugar
1 C pineapple juice
3 TB wine vinegar
½ tsp salt
1 TB cornstarch
2 TB water
1 C pineapple chunks
1 green or red pepper chopped fine
4 TB minced pickled red ginger (optional)

In a saucepan bring to a boil ketchup, sugar, pineapple juice, vinegar and salt. Blend cornstarch and water and add to mixture. Cook until thick. Add peppers and pineapple chunks.

TO USE WON TON IN SOUP: Bring 3 qt water to a boil. Add about 15-20 filled won tons. When they float to the top, add 1 C cold water. Bring to a boil again. When they float to the top again they are ready for use in soup. Remove with slotted spoon. Add to heated chicken broth. Add a few bok choy leaves, green onions and drops of sesame oil.

minced meat in lettuce cups

An inspired use of crisp, green lettuce leaves instead of high calorie crepes

4 oz rice stick noodles (mai fun)
2 C oil for deep frying
½ head iceberg lettuce
¼ lb chicken livers
½ lb ground lean beef
½ C chopped mushrooms or 1 pkg dried forest
    mushrooms (preferred but expensive)
2 green onions, white part only, chopped fine
1 C water chestnuts, chopped fine
1 TB imitation bacon bits
½ tsp minced fresh ginger root
2 cloves garlic, minced
½ tsp sugar
1 TB bean sauce
1 TB soy sauce
½ tsp oriental sesame oil

Soak forest mushrooms in warm water for 20 minutes. Squeeze dry and chop. Heat 2 C oil in wok until very hot. Test with one noodle until it puffs. If it turns brown, the oil is too hot. Separate noodles. Deep fry ½ handful at a time only 1-2 seconds. Remove with wire skimmer and drain on paper towel. Crush lightly. Strain oil into a container, reserving ¼ C. Wash lettuce leaves individually. Drain and chill.

Measure and mix together sugar, bean sauce, soy sauce and sesame oil. Heat ¼ C oil in a large frying pan. Stir fry chicken livers. Set aside and chop. Stir fry beef, then add onions, water chestnuts, imitation bacon bits, ginger root, garlic, mixed seasonings and chicken livers. Cook and stir together until all flavors are blended. Add a little more soy sauce if needed for taste.

Place a lettuce cup on each plate. Place noodles in cup. Spoon beef mixture over noodles. Serve immediately. Guests will fold leaf together and eat filled cup with their hands. Serves 4 as appetizer.

glazed chicken wings

Finger likin' good

3 lb chicken wings (about 15 wings)
¼ C soy sauce
¼ C dry sherry
¼ C vinegar
2 cloves garlic, crushed
¼ tsp ground ginger
½ tsp salt
½ tsp oriental sesame oil
¼ C honey
3 TB sesame seeds, optional

Cut tips off each wing, and cut each wing in two pieces. Combine soy sauce, sherry, vinegar, garlic, ginger and oil. Marinate wings in this mixture overnight.

Pour marinade into a small saucepan. Add honey. Simmer for 10 minutes. Place wings in a baking pan. Bake in a 375 degree oven about 1 hour, basting with the sauce until they are brown and glazed. Remove from oven and sprinkle with sesame seeds.

pea pods with mushrooms

½ lb pea pods
½ lb fresh mushrooms
1 6-oz can water chestnuts
1 tsp salt
½ tsp sugar
2 TB chicken stock
1 TB soy sauce
1 TB cornstarch
2 TB water
2 TB oil

Wash and drain pea pods. Drain water chestnuts, and cut in half. Wash and slice mushrooms. In one dish blend salt, sugar and stock. In another dish blend soy sauce, cornstarch and water. Heat oil in wok. Stir fry pea pods for one minute. Remove. Stir fry mushrooms 1 minute. Combine vegetables, stock mixture, then add cornstarch mixture. Heat thoroughly until vegetables are glazed.

beef and asparagus

Expensive ingredients go a long way in this flavorful dish

1 lb lean beef
1 TB cornstarch
½ tsp salt
4 TB oil
½ lb fresh asparagus*
1 TB sherry
2 TB hoisin sauce
1 TB soy sauce
4 TB chicken stock or beef stock
1 tsp sugar
3 cloves garlic, minced
1 tsp minced fresh ginger root
1 stalk green onion, cut in strips

Slice beef, while partially frozen into thin ⅛" x 1½" long slices. Marinade in mixture of cornstarch and salt for 20 minutes. Cut asparagus diagonally into pieces 2" long. In a dish, mix sherry, hoisin sauce, soy sauce, stock and sugar.

Heat 2 TB oil in wok until very hot. Stir fry minced ginger and garlic for ½ a minute. Remove from wok. Stir fry asparagus 2-3 minutes. Remove. Stir fry onions, 2 minutes. Remove. Add 2 more TB oil. When oil is hot, stir fry the beef for 3 minutes. Add sauce and vegetables and cook until heated thoroughly. Serve immediately.

*Broccoli may be substituted for asparagus.

egg foo yung puffs

1 C bean sprouts
¼ C chopped onion
4 water chestnuts
3-4 eggs
1 tsp sherry
1 tsp salt
1 TB soy sauce
2 C oil

Chop bean sprouts, onions and water chestnuts. Stir fry bean sprouts and onion in 2 TB hot oil. Drain well. Heat rest of oil. Scramble eggs with sherry, salt and soy sauce. Add vegetables.

Drop by ½ a soup ladle into hot oil. As they puff up turn over and remove immediately. Drain on paper towel. Serve with egg foo yung sauce.

EGG FOO YUNG SAUCE
1 C chicken stock
1 TB soy sauce
pepper to taste
2 tsp sherry
1 TB cornstarch
2 TB water

Boil stock, soy sauce, pepper and sherry together. Blend cornstarch and water. Add to stock. Cook until thick and clear. Serve over egg foo yung. Sprinkle with chopped green onions (optional).

korean marinade

Great for ribs or barbeque beef

2 C soy sauce
½ C sugar
¼ C oil
1 tsp oriental sesame oil
1 tsp pepper
3 cloves garlic
1 C green onions, finely chopped
3 TB sesame seeds, optional

fried noodles

One night its elegant "grenadine of beef",
the next day you economize with fried noodles

1 lb rice noodles, egg noodles or thin vermicelli
1 TB oil
1 lb ground meat or any left over cooked chicken or meat
2½ TB oil
2 cloves garlic, chopped fine
1 medium onion chopped
4 carrots, thinly sliced
4 stalks celery, thinly sliced
4 stalks bok choy, sliced
2-3 eggs
salt and pepper to taste
soy sauce to taste

Heat 8-9 C water to a boil. Put in noodles and cook for 5 minutes until barely tender. Drain and immediately mix with 1 Tb oil and salt and pepper. Saute ground beef until well done. Season with salt and pepper. Set aside.

In the same pan saute onion and garlic in 2½ TB oil. When the onion is golden add the carrots. When the carrots are just tender add the ground beef. Push everything aside. Scramble the eggs in the same pan. Add celery, bok choy and noodles. Mix all together. Correct seasoning, adding as much soy sauce as desired. Serves 4-6.

spinach with bean curd (to-fu)

To-fu is made from pureed soybeans.
It is nutritiously high in protein but low in fat.

2 TB oil
2 large bunches spinach
1 cake fresh to-fu (bean curd)
2 TB soy sauce
½ C chicken stock
1 TB chili paste, optional

Heat oil in wok. Quickly stir fry washed and well drained spinach leaves. Cut bean curd into bite size pieces. Add to spinach. Add soy sauce and chicken stock. Heat thoroughly. Serve with rice.

crispy duck

*This may seem complicated, but its worth discovering
another delicious way to serve duck*

4-5 lb duck
4 green onions
3 large slices fresh ginger
4 garlic cloves
pepper to taste
2 TB soy sauce
½ C flour
4 C oil
Hoisin Sauce or Chinese plum sauce

Wash duck and trim excess fat. Score skin in fatty areas. Fill cavity with green onions, ginger and garlic. Sprinkle pepper sparingly on top. To steam, place a rack in a roasting pan with water up to the rack. Simmer covered on top of the stove for 1-1½ hours until almost tender. Cool and baste with soy sauce. Wrap in foil and marinate in the refrigerator overnight.

The next day, remove vegetables from the cavity. Bring to room temperature. Coat outside with flour, shaking off excess. Heat oil in wok until very hot. Fry each side until golden and crispy. Drain on paper towels. To make duck very crisp repeat frying whole duck. Drain again on paper towels. Serve whole, or cut into bite size pieces. Serve with hoisin or plum sauce or duck sauce.

DUCK SAUCE
½ C apple sauce
½ C apricot jam
½ C plum jam
½ C orange marmalade
½ tsp minced garlic
½ tsp minced ginger
a pinch of dried red chili, optional

Blend in a processor. Keeps well refrigerated.

beef and onions

A flavorful dish that can be prepared in minutes

1 lb lean beef
2 TB sherry
2 TB soy sauce
1 tsp sugar
1 tsp oil
2 tsp cornstarch
2 TB oil
3 cloves garlic, minced
2 C thinly sliced onions
1 C thinly sliced green pepper
1 C sliced mushrooms

Slice beef into julienne strips 2" long. Marinate in mixture of sherry, soy sauce, sugar, oil and cornstarch for 20 minutes. Slice onions and green pepper into same size strips.

Heat 2 TB oil in wok. Stir fry garlic, do not burn. Remove from wok. Stir fry onion, then green pepper, then mushrooms. Remove from wok. Heat 2 TB oil. Stir fry beef. Add vegetables, and stir all together. Add more soy sauce to taste.

If more gravy is desired, in a separate small pan combine 1 TB soy sauce, 1 TB cornstarch and ½ C beef broth. Add to beef and heat thoroughly.

chicken walnut or cashew

Make your favorite restaurant dish at home

1½ lb chicken breasts, cut in bite size pieces
1 tsp salt
1 egg white
1 TB cornstarch
2 C oil for deep frying*
1 C walnuts or cashews
1 C celery, cut diagonally in ½" pieces
2 TB bean sauce
2 TB sugar
4 TB chicken stock

Mix the raw chicken pieces with salt, egg white and cornstarch. Heat oil in wok. Deep fry chicken pieces until they turn white. Fry nuts. Drain on paper towels. Cool oil and strain into a container to be used again. Heat 1 TB oil and stir fry celery for 1 minute. Remove. Heat 2 TB oil in wok and add bean sauce. Stir until hot. Add sugar and stock. Cook together until hot and add chicken and celery. Sprinkle fried nuts on top and serve at once with rice.

*The deep frying gives a delicate crisp texture to the chicken.

teriyaki beef buns

Great for a crowd of teenagers or an "after theater" supper party

2 lb thinly sliced lean beef
1 TB fresh grated ginger
2 cloves garlic, chopped
1 medium onion, minced
2 TB sugar
¼ C soy sauce
¼ C sherry
¼ C water

Thinly slice beef while partially frozen. Mix all ingredients together. Marinate beef for 2 hours at room temperature. Drain marinade off. Spread beef in a shallow pan and broil for 3-5 minutes on each side, or barbeque. Serve in buns or rolls with lettuce and tomatoes. Enough for 8-10 sandwiches, depending on appetites.

suki

Bring to the table and make it the centerpiece of your menu

1½ lb lean beef, thinly sliced
2 TB oil
4 TB sugar
1 C soy sauce
1 C chicken broth or mushroom liquid
   from the canned mushrooms
5 green onions, cut 1½" length pieces
½ lb fresh spinach, washed and dried
2 medium onions, sliced
1 8-oz can mushrooms, or fresh mushrooms
½ C canned bamboo shoots, drained
1 C celery, sliced diagonally
1 8-oz can water chestnuts, drained and sliced

Saute beef in oil. Add sugar, stirring for 2-3 minutes. Add ½ C soy sauce. Cook 3 minutes. Add rest of ingredients. Cook a few minutes just to heat thoroughly. Serve with rice or Japanese noodles.

chinese almond cookies

3 C flour
1 tsp baking soda
½ tsp salt
¾ C butter or margarine
1 C sugar
1 egg
1 tsp almond extract
¾ C vegetable oil
1 C blanched whole almonds
1 egg yolk for glaze

Sift flour, baking soda and salt together. In a mixing bowl cream butter with sugar until light. Add egg and almond extract and mix thoroughly. Gradually add dry ingredients, alternating with vegetable oil, starting with flour, then oil, and always ending with flour.

Drop 1 TB of batter on a lightly greased cookie sheet. Allow room for expansion. Brush with beaten egg yolk. Press whole almond into top of each cookie. Bake at 350 degrees for 12-15 minutes. Check after 10 minutes. Keep cookies light in color, but bottoms should be lightly browned. Remove and cool on rack. Makes about 60 cookies.

fruit compote

Serve as a light dessert, with duck and other main courses

1 can* pineapple or fresh
1 can lichee nuts
1 can mandarin oranges
1 can kumquats
¼ C Grand Marnier or Kirsch

Drain cans of fruit. Mix with liqueur. Let blend for at least 6 hours. Strawberries, kiwis and bananas may also be added, or arrange fruit pieces on skewers on a pretty platter.

*vary amounts according to taste

filled won ton crispies

1 C raisins steeped in apple juice and
    drained, or 1 C chopped dates
1 C chopped tart apples
½ C chopped nuts
rind of 1 lemon
2 TB lemon juice
1 TB light Karo syrup
½ TB cornstarch
1 pkg won ton skins (thin ones preferred)
4 C oil for deep frying
powdered sugar

Chop raisins, apples and nuts together. Mix well with lemon rind, juice, syrup and cornstarch. Put a level teaspoon of filling in one corner of each wonton skin, floured side on the outside. Moisten edges with finger dipped in water. Fold point over and seal. Roll and pinch ends. It will look like a wrapped piece of candy. Heat oil. Deep fry until golden. Drain on paper towels. Sprinkle with powdered sugar.

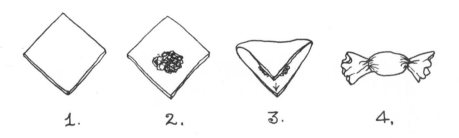

1.   2.   3.   4.

won ton crispies

1 pkg won ton skins
2 C oil
powdered sugar

Cut won ton in half and separate. In deep frying pan or wok heat oil until it sizzles. Deep fry a few at a time, turning once until golden brown. Drain on paper towels. Sprinkle with powdered sugar. If any are left over store in airtight container.

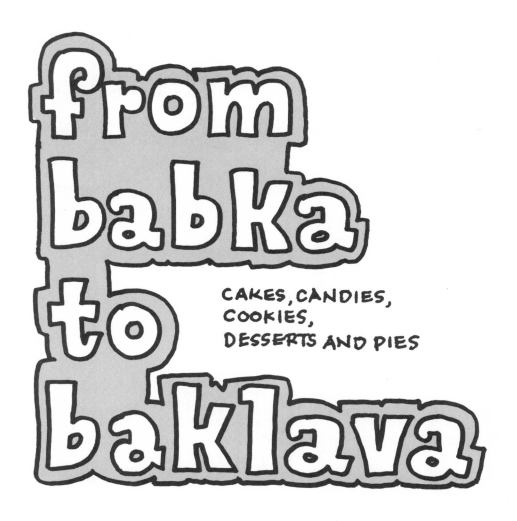

from babka to baklava

CAKES, CANDIES,
COOKIES,
DESSERTS AND PIES

antebellum fruit cake

Good to the last crumb

¼ lb butter
1 C sugar
4 eggs, separated
1 C flour
¼ tsp salt
1 tsp baking powder
½ C cold coffee
½ C whiskey
Candied fruit and nuts cut up into small pieces:
4 oz each of red, green and natural pineapple
4 oz citron
4 oz candied lemon peel, cut fine
4 oz candied orange peel, cut fine
4 oz white raisins
4 oz dark raisins
4 oz walnuts
4 oz pecans

2 oz brazil nuts
2 oz almonds
4 oz pitted dates
1 tsp cinnamon
½ tsp allspice
½ tsp cloves
½ tsp nutmeg
½ tsp mace

Cream butter and beat in sugar. Beat in egg yolks one at a time. Sift ½ C flour with salt and baking powder and add alternately with coffee and whiskey. Sprinkle ½ C flour over chopped fruits and nuts and mix. Add to batter. Beat egg whites and fold into mixture.

Line angel food pan or bundt pan with brown paper, which has been oiled. Bake at 250 degrees for about 2 hours. Test with toothpick for doneness. Cool for 30 minutes. Loosen edges with a knife and turn out on cake rack. When cold, wrap in foil and store in tin cookie can or casserole which have covers.

Sprinkle stored fruit cake with whiskey or brandy once a week until used. Flavor improves if aged at least two weeks. Can be baked in loaf pans then stored and covered with foil.

apple cream cake

2 C zweiback crumbs
4 TB melted butter
2 TB sugar
2 tsp cinnamon
6 large pippin apples
3 TB butter
3 TB sugar
6 eggs
1 C sugar
1 pint sour cream
1 tsp grated lemon rind
½ pint whipped cream, optional

Combine crumbs, butter, sugar and cinnamon. Using 1½ C of crumbs, press onto bottom and sides of a 9″ spring form pan. Refrigerate to harden. Péel and slice apples. Simmer in a saucepan with butter and sugar until tender.

Beat eggs, sugar and sour cream and lemon peel together. Add to apples slowly, watching that cream does not curdle. Simmer very slowly over low heat for 2 minutes. Pour into chilled crust. Top with remaining crumbs. Bake at 375 degrees for 45 minutes. Serve at room temperature with whipped cream. Serves 12-14.

jelly roll

½ tsp cream of tartar
6 eggs, separated
1 C sugar
1C flour
½ tsp baking powder
½ tsp vanilla
1 C any kind of jelly you prefer

Add cream of tartar to egg whites and beat until stiff. Add sugar and continue beating until mixture looks like marshmallows. Beat yolks. Sift flour and baking powder and fold into egg mixture. Add vanilla. Fold in whites.

Line a cookie pan or 15 x 12 inch jelly roll pan with wax paper. Put mixture into pan. Bake 15 minutes at 350 degrees or until toothpick comes out clean.

Remove cake to towel and sprinkle with powdered sugar. Place strawberry or blueberry jelly at edge of jelly roll and roll up using towel.

apple strudel

CRUST*
3 large eggs or 4 small ones
½ C honey
½ tsp salt
1 tsp baking soda
½ C peanut oil
2 C flour
¼ C warm water

FILLING
2½ lb pippin apples, sliced
1 TB cinnamon
6 tsp sugar
2 TB peanut oil
1 pt jar peach or apricot and pineapple preserves
1 pt jar strawberry preserves
½ C chopped nuts
1 C cornflakes, crushed

CRUST: Mix all ingredients in mixer, using 1½ C of the flour. Then knead by hand and keep adding the rest of the flour. Roll out 2 sheets of dough about ⅛" thick.

FILLING: Peel, core and slice apples thinly. Add the sugar and cinnamon. Use more sugar if apples are tart. Brush oil over the dough and on one side place row of apples, then some of each of the preserves and ½ of the nuts. Then sprinkle the crushed cornflakes over the whole sheet. Begin to roll the strudel, tucking in the sides as you go. Place on greased cookie sheet with the seam side down. Repeat process with other sheet of dough. Bake at 350 degrees for 25-35 minutes. Remove from oven and score into serving pieces. Return to oven and bake for another 12 minutes. Can be frozen.

*Filo leaves may be used

apricot cake

6 oz butter
¾ C sugar
3 eggs, separated
juice and rind of 1 lemon
1½ C flour
2 tsp baking powder
¾ C milk
1½-2 lb fresh apricots, pitted and halved*

Cream butter, add sugar and egg yolks and cream until thick and yellow in color. Add lemon juice and rind, flour, baking powder and milk. When well mixed, fold in beaten egg whites. Pour in 9″ greased springform.

Place apricots in circles, starting with a row closest to side. Do not push fruit down, but insert into batter at an angle about ½″ from top of batter.

As cake bakes, fruit will sink to the bottom. You may not need full 2 lb to complete rows. Bake in preheated oven at 375 degrees for 1 hour and 15 minutes or until wooden pick comes out clean when tested.

*or 1½ lb drained pitted sour cherries or 1½ lb canned apricots, drained and pitted

brandied apple cake

An apple a day should be served this way

6 TB brandy
4 C apples, chopped (6-8)
3 eggs
½ C oil
2 C sugar
2 C flour
¼ C nuts, chopped
1 C raisins
2 tsp cinnamon
2 tsp baking soda
1 tsp nutmeg
1/3 tsp salt
¼ tsp ground cloves

Pour brandy over chopped apples. In another bowl beat eggs. Add oil and sugar. Combine flour, nuts, raisins, cinnamon, baking soda, nutmeg, salt and ground cloves. Mix everything together and pour into greased 9 x 13 pan. Bake about 1 hour at 325 degrees.

old fashioned cheese cake

Once in a while, a taste you deserve

BOTTOM CRUST
2 C graham cracker crumbs
4 TB ground walnuts
2 TB sugar
¼ lb melted butter

Mix together. Butter a 9″ x 3″ spring form pan. Pat crumbs on bottom and sides. Bake at 350 degrees for 10 minutes.

CAKE
1 lb cream cheese, at room temperature
1 C sugar
6 eggs, separated
1 lb sour cream
1 C milk
3 TB flour
⅛ tsp salt
1 tsp vanilla
2-4 TB fresh lemon juice

Cream the cheese. Add sugar, reserving 3 TB. Add egg yolks, sour cream, milk, flour, salt, vanilla and lemon juice. Beat egg whites with 3 TB sugar. Fold into cheese mixture. Pour into pan. Bake at 350 degrees for 1 hour 15 minutes. Turn heat off. Leave in oven 1 hour and 15 minutes, leaving oven door partially open. Cool and refrigerate. May be frozen.

chocolate chip sour cream cake

    1 pkg yellow cake mix
    ¾ C water
    1 C sour cream
    2 eggs
    6 oz chocolate chips, coarsely crushed
    3 TB instant cocoa mix

In electric mixer beat together cake mix, water, sour cream and eggs. Beat at medium speed for 4 minutes. Add chocolate chips and mix until blended.

Place ½ batter in greased and floured 9″ angel food pan. Sprinkle chocolate powder evenly over the batter. Pour remaining batter evenly over chocolate powder. With scraper, cut into batter to marbelize. Bake at 325 degrees for 50 minutes. Can be dusted with powdered sugar when cool.

low calorie no bake cheesecake

No baking and hardly any calories, what could be better

CRUST: Place graham crackers (16) in the blender and whiz until fine. Melt ¼ C butter and stir into graham cracker crumbs. Press into 9″ pie pan.

    2 TB cold water
    2 TB lemon juice
    1 envelope unflavored gelatin
    ½ C milk
    1 whole egg
    1/3 C sugar
    1 tsp vanilla flavoring
    2 C low-fat cottage cheese

Put cold water, lemon juice and gelatin into blender, cover and whiz at lowest speed for two to three seconds to soften ingredients. Remove top of blender, add boiling milk while blender is in motion. Turn off blender and with rubber spatula scrape down the food from the sides of blender. Replace top and turn blender to highest setting.

Add egg, sugar, vanilla and cottage cheese and continue to process until smooth. Pour immediately into prepared pie shell of your choice. Refrigerate one or two hours until firm. Serve plain or with frozen topping and fruit.

louisiana apple cake

3 C delicious apples, peeled and
    chopped to size of peas
1 TB lemon juice
1 TB grated lemon rind
1 C pecans, chopped
2½ C flour
1¼ tsp baking soda
1 tsp salt
1 tsp cinnamon
¼ tsp nutmeg
⅛ tsp mace, optional
2 C sugar
1¼ C oil
2 tsp vanilla
2 large eggs
¼ C sifted powdered sugar (to dust baked cake)

Put chopped apples in a bowl with lemon juice, grated lemon rind and pecans. Sift flour before measuring. Sift flour together with soda, salt, cinnamon, nutmeg and mace. Combine sugar, oil, vanilla and eggs in a large bowl of electric mixer. Beat at medium speed, about 1 minute. Turn to low speed and add sifted flour mixture, beating no more than 2 minutes. As quickly as possible stir in apple and pecan mixture by hand. The batter will be thick.

Grease and flour a bundt pan. (Do not use oil). Pour batter into pan. Bake at 350 degrees about 1½ hours. Cool on wire rack before removing cake from pan. Dust cake with powdered sugar.

eggnog cake

1 pkg yellow cake mix
1 3-oz vanilla instant pudding
4 eggs
¾ C oil
¾ C sherry wine
1 tsp nutmeg

Blend all ingredients in mixer for 3 to 4 minutes. Bake in a bundt pan, which has been oiled and sugared, at 350 degrees for about 50-60 minutes. Sprinkle with powdered sugar if desired.

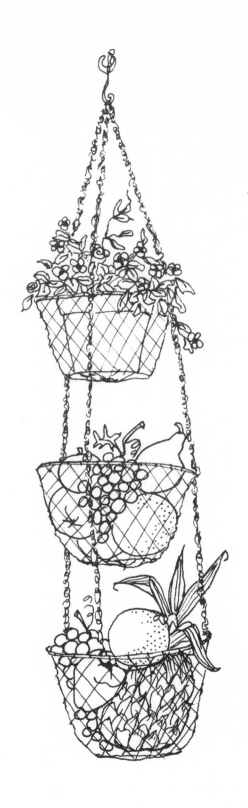

sunken fruit cake

A sunken treasure

1 lb peaches, blueberries, cherries (canned sour)
    apples or plums, fresh or canned
3 eggs
1 C sugar
3½ oz butter, melted
1¼ C flour
1½ tsp baking powder
¾ tsp vanilla
2 oz slivered almonds

Beat eggs and sugar until light. Add melted butter mixing well. Combine flour and baking powder. Add to batter. Add vanilla. Pour into greased 12″ pyrex pie plate or 9″ spring form. Put fruit into batter. Sprinkle with chopped nuts, or slivered almonds.

Bake in 350 degree oven about 1 hour depending on fruit used. Sprinkle with powdered sugar (optional).

pumpkin cake

Great for a crowd

1 29-oz can pumpkin, solid packed (about 3 C)
4 beaten eggs
1½ C sugar
½ tsp salt
1 TB cinnamon
1 tsp nutmeg
½ tsp ground ginger
13 oz can evaporated milk
1 box yellow cake mix
1 C chopped nuts
¼ lb sweet butter

Mix pumpkin, eggs, sugar, salt, cinnamon, nutmeg, ginger and milk thoroughly. Pour into a 9″ x 13″ pyrex baking pan. Cover with 1 box yellow cake mix, sprinkled directly from the box. Top with chopped nuts. Drizzle melted butter over top. Bake at 325 degrees 1 hour and 20 minutes. Cool in the oven.

peanut butter bundt cake

½ C finely chopped peanuts
1 pkg yellow cake mix
1 pkg, 3¾ oz instant vanilla pudding mix
1¼ C water
½ C oil
4 eggs
1 C peanut butter
1 C soft dates, cut up
½ C semi-sweet chocolate pieces

Generously grease a 10″ bundt pan with softened butter. Sprinkle chopped peanuts in pan. Shake pan to coat surface with nuts.

In mixing bowl beat cake and pudding mix, water, oil and eggs until well blended, about 4 minutes on medium speed. Beat in peanut butter. Pour 1/3 of the batter into pan. Sprinkle with layers of dates and chocolate pieces.

Repeat, pouring remaining batter into pan and bake at 350 degrees about 55 minutes or until cake tests done. Cool cake in pan about 25 minutes then turn out on a rack to cool. Drizzle lemon icing or serve with ice cream balls.

LEMON ICING
¼ C lemon juice
1 C powdered sugar

chocolate marble cake

¼ lb plus 2 TB butter
1 C sugar
5 eggs, separated
1½ C flour
2 tsp baking powder
¼ C slightly warmed milk
3 oz semi-sweet chocolate

Cream butter. Add sugar and egg yolks. Beat until you have a creamy light yellow consistency. Add flour, baking powder and milk reserving 1 TB milk. Melt chocolate and 1 TB milk on top of double boiler. Separate batter into 2 parts. Mix chocolate into 1 part.

Beat egg whites and add evenly into each ½ of the batter. Pour two batters alternately into greased loaf pan 9 x 5 x 2. Cut batter with a knife to get marble effect. Bake in 350 degree oven 45-50 minutes. Cool. Delicious as is, or frost with your favorite chocolate frosting.

173

babka

No need to knead
Make the batter a day ahead. The secret is the light touch.
Serve right out of the oven to your delighted guests.

½ lb butter or margarine
2/3 C sugar
1 pkg dry yeast
3 TB warm water
3 eggs, beaten
1 C half and half
4 C flour
½ C chopped nuts
½ C raisins
½ C sugar mixed with 2 TB cinnamon
¼ lb frozen butter or margarine in small chips

Cream butter and sugar. Dissolve yeast in warm water. Add beaten eggs and cream. Alternately add liquid mixture and flour to sugar-butter mixture. Blend with a fork. *Do not over mix.* Cover with a damp towel, and refrigerate overnight.

Take out of refrigerator, and bring to room temperature. Roll dough on floured board with floured rolling pin. Make filling by mixing nuts, raisins, sugar mixture and butter. Spread filling evenly on rolled dough. Roll up forming one long cylinder. Place in greased tube pan, pinch the two ends together. Bake at 350 degrees about 50 minutes, until the aroma drives you crazy. Test with toothpick in the center.

chocolate browny cake

¼ lb butter
2 C sugar
6 eggs, beaten well
4 oz bitter chocolate, melted
1 TB vanilla
2 C cake flour, sifted
2 tsp baking powder
2 C nuts, chopped and lightly floured

Cream butter, add sugar and beaten eggs. Add melted chocolate and vanilla. Sift flour with baking powder. Add to mixture and add nuts. Bake in greased 9″ x 13″ pan at 350 degrees for 25 minutes. Do not overbake. Cut while warm.

chocolate cheese cake

Some things just naturally go together

CRUST
1 box chocolate ice box cookies
**   crushed to make 2 C crumbs**
¼ lb melted butter
3 TB sugar
½ tsp nutmeg

Combine ingredients. Spread on bottom and sides of a 9 x 3 spring form pan. Chill.

CAKE
1 lb cream cheese
½ lb ricotta cheese
1 C sugar
6 eggs, separated
1 pt sour cream
½ C imported Dutch cocoa
2 TB cake flour
1 TB plus 1 tsp vanilla
1 TB plus 1 tsp coffee liqueur

In large bowl of electric mixer beat cheeses together until creamy. Add sugar, egg yolks and sour cream beating thoroughly after each addition. Add cocoa, flour, vanilla and liqueur. Beat egg whites until stiff but not dry. Gently fold beaten egg whites into mixture. Bake at 325 degrees for one hour. Turn oven off.

Leave cake in the oven with the door closed 1 hour longer. Cool. Remove sides of pan. May be served at room temperature or chilled. May be made a day ahead. May be frozen. May be garnished with whipped cream.

frostings

SOUR CREAM/LEMON
2 TB soft butter or margarine
2½-3 C powdered sugar
¼ C sour cream
⅛ tsp salt
1½ TB lemon juice
½ tsp grated lemon peel

Cream butter and sugar. Add sour cream, salt, lemon juice and lemon peel. Beat until fluffy. Refrigerate cake after frosting.

CREAM CHEESE FROSTING
1 lb powdered sugar
½ C butter
8 oz cream cheese
1 tsp vanilla

Blend all ingredients until smooth.

CHOCOLATE FROSTING
¼ lb plus 4 TB butter
3 oz unsweetened chocolate
5 TB imported cocoa
1¼ lb powdered sugar
1 TB vanilla
1 TB sweet cream
½-¾ C hot coffee

Blend all together using as much coffee as needed to make a smooth icing. This amount is enough for a 9″ layer cake plus 10 cupcakes. The quality of the cocoa makes the difference.

homemade pancake syrup

1 C granulated sugar
1 C light brown sugar
1 C boiling water
½ tsp imitation maple flavoring

Put sugar in a pan. Pour in the boiling water. Boil gently for 10-15 minutes. Remove from heat and add the maple flavoring. Its "pourfectly" simple.

plum cake

(PFLAUMEN KUCHEN)

Out of this world from the old world

40 Italian plums
¾ C sugar
1 tsp cinnamon
½ tsp nutmeg
½ lb butter
2 eggs
2 C flour
½ tsp baking powder
½ tsp vanilla or almond extract

TOPPING
1 egg
1 C warmed milk
2 tsp sugar
½ tsp vanilla or almond extract

Slice plums in half. Discard pits. Mix with ¼ C sugar, cinnamon and nutmeg to taste. Set aside. Cream butter, add remaining sugar, eggs and vanilla. Beat well. Combine flour and baking powder. Add to butter mixture. Butter 9" x 13" pyrex pan. Spread dough on bottom and sides. Place plums on top.

Mix egg, warmed milk, sugar and vanilla. Pour topping over all. Bake in 350 degree oven at least 30 minutes or until crust is light brown.

baklava

A taste of honey and all good things

1 lb pkg filo leaves
1 lb melted butter or margarine
1 lb finely chopped walnuts
grated peel of one orange
2 tsp cinnamon
1 tsp nutmeg
½ tsp ground cloves

SYRUP
2 C sugar
2 C water
3 TB lemon juice
3″ cinnamon stick
6 whole cloves
½ C honey

Mix nuts, spices and orange peel. Brush bottom and sides of a pan 15″ x 10″ with melted butter. Unfold filo leaves. Cover with wax paper and damp towel to keep from drying out. Cut leaves to fit size of pan.

Place 2 leaves on bottom of pan. Brush with butter. Sprinkle with nut mixture. Repeat, alternating 2 leaves and nut mixture until all leaves and nuts are used up, covering top with 2 filo leaves. With sharp knife cut through first nut layer making diagonal pieces 1½″ x 2″. Pour remaining butter over top. May be frozen up to this point. (Do not freeze after baking) Bake at 350 degrees for 30 minutes. Then at 300 degrees for 45 minutes.

Meanwhile make syrup. Boil sugar and water, lemon juice, cinnamon stick and cloves together for 5-7 minutes. Remove from heat. Discard cinnamon and cloves. Stir in honey. Cool.

When Baklava is baked, place pan on wire rack. Pour cooled syrup over top. Cool. Cut along scored lines to the bottom. Makes 42 pieces.

banana cake

Moist and chewy

2 C sugar
3 eggs
1 tsp vanilla
¼ lb margarine or butter, melted
3 ripe bananas
2 C cake flour, sifted
2 tsp baking soda
dash salt
½ pt sour cream
1 C nuts, ground or chopped

Cream sugar and eggs. Add vanilla, melted butter, and bananas. Mix well. Alternate flour sifted with soda and salt and sour cream. Add nuts. Grease and flour 2 9″ x 9″ aluminum pans. Bake in 325 degree oven for 45 minutes.

chocolate mousse cake

(molded)

5 oz semi-sweet chocolate
                    or
¾ C chocolate, semi-sweet chips
¼ C strong coffee
7 eggs, separated
¼ C sugar
1 tsp vanilla
⅛ tsp salt
Ladyfingers

Grease an 8″ spring form pan. Melt chocolate in top of double boiler over not quite boiling water. Add coffee and cool. Beat egg yolks until thick, then beat in sugar and vanilla. Beat together chocolate and egg yolk mixtures. Add salt to egg whites and beat gently. Spoon into mold. Chill.

Variation: Line spring form with lady fingers. Pour half of moussee into mold, then top with layer of lady fingers. Pour remaining mousse over all. Chill. May be garnished with whipping cream.

crunchy chocolate date cake

The dates give a moist texture and the
candy bars are a topping surprise

1 10-oz pkg dates, cut up
1 C boiling water
1 tsp baking soda
¼ lb sweet butter
1 C sugar, sifted
2 eggs, beaten
1 tsp vanilla
2 tsp cocoa
1 1/3 C flour, sifted
8 1-oz chocolate almond candy bars*

Pour boiling water over dates and stir. Add baking soda, stir and cool. Cream butter and sugar. Add eggs, vanilla, cocoa. Alternate flour and date mixture. Pour into buttered 9″ x 9″ baking pan. Top with crumbled candy bars. Bake at 350 degrees for 40 minutes.

*You must use small bars for the correct texture.

sicilian chocolate cake (cassata)

Bravo, bravo, bravo, and the frosting is terrific too

1 fresh pound cake loaf (about 9 x 5 x 3)
1 lb ricotta cheese
2 TB heavy cream
¼ C sugar
3 TB orange liqueur
3 TB coarsely chopped candied fruit (optional)
2 oz semi-sweet chocolate, grated

Cut ends and level top of the pound cake. Cut cake horizontally into 3 layers. Beat cheese until smooth. Add cream, sugar and liqueur. Fold in candied fruit and grated chocolate. Spread mixture between layers. Press together to compact. Refrigerate 2 hours to firm.

FROSTING
8 oz semi-sweet chocolate, broken into pieces
½ C strong black coffee
¼ lb sweet butter, cut into ½″ pieces and chilled

Melt the chocolate with the coffee in a double boiler, over low heat, stirring constantly. Remove from heat and beat in the chilled butter one piece at a time until smooth. Chill until thick enough to spread, about 1 hour. Frost cake. Chill. Cover with plastic wrap and refrigerate for at least 24 hours.

chocolate mayonnaise cake

An unbelievably rich tasting, moist cake that you can serve with a meat dinner

2 C unsifted flour
2/3 C unsweetened cocoa
¼ tsp baking powder
1¼ tsp baking soda
1 2/3 C sugar
3 eggs
1 tsp vanilla
1 C real mayonnaise
1 1/3 C water
6 oz chocolate chips

Grease and flour the bottom of two 8″ round cake pans. In a medium bowl stir together flour, cocoa, baking powder and baking soda and set aside. In a large bowl with mixer at high speed, beat sugar, eggs and vanilla, occasionally scraping the bowl, for 3 minutes or until light and fluffy. Reduce speed to low. Beat in mayonnaise.

Add flour mixture in 4 additions, alternately with water, beginning and ending with flour. Blend chocolate chips into mixture. Pour into pans. Bake in 350 degree oven for 30-35 minutes or until cake tester inserted in center comes out clean. Remove from oven and cool on wire racks. Frost with chocolate frosting.

chocolate syrup cake

¼ lb butter or margarine
1 C sugar
4 eggs
1 C flour
1½ tsp baking powder
1 16-oz can chocolate syrup
1 tsp vanilla
1 C nuts, chopped

Cream butter and sugar. Add eggs. Sift flour with baking powder and slowly add to mixture. Add syrup, vanilla and nuts. Bake in 8″ x 8″ buttered pan at 350 degrees for 50-55 minutes. Cool and frost or sift powdered sugar on top.

chocolate truffles

12 oz semi-sweet chocolate
4 egg yolks
4 TB milk
2 tsp coffee or orange liqueur
6 TB sweet butter

Melt chocolate in a double boiler. Add egg yolks one at a time stirring vigorously for a few seconds after each addition. Remove from heat. Add milk, coffee and place back on heat for a few seconds, stirring constantly. The mixture should be smooth. Remove from heat. Transfer to an electric mixer. Add butter, bit by bit, beating constantly, to let mixture absorb air and become fluffy. Cover with plastic wrap and refrigerate until firm. (Can freeze at this point). Roll into balls. Roll in bitter cocoa or dip in melted chocolate. Place on wax paper and refrigerate. Must be kep in the refrigerator.

peanut truffles

They look pretty in ruffled paper candy cases

1 C butter or margarine
2 C finely crushed graham crackers
1 tsp vanilla
1 C coconut flakes
1 1-lb box powdered sugar
1 C chunk-style peanut butter
1 lb semi-sweet chocolate

Beat butter in a large mixing bowl until creamy. Grind coconut coarsely in processor. Add graham cracker crumbs, vanilla, coconut, sugar and mix thoroughly. Stir in peanut butter. Shape into 1″ balls and place on wax paper lined baking sheet. Refrigerate 1 hour. Melt chocolate in a double boiler, over simmering water. Dip peanut balls and swirl in chocolate. Place on wax paper to harden. Store in refrigerator. Makes 8 dozen truffles.

divinity

2 C sugar
1 TB vinegar
½ C white corn syrup
¼ tsp salt
1/3 C hot water
2 egg whites
½ tsp vanilla
½ C nuts, coarsely chopped
1/3 C candied cherries, minced
1/3 C candied pineapple

Combine sugar, vinegar, syrup, salt and water in sauce pan, cook and stir until sugar is dissolved. Continue cooking without stirring until small amount forms a hard ball when dropped into iced water. Remove from heat and very slowly pour mixture over stiffly beaten egg whites. Beat constantly. Add vanilla, nuts and fruits last. Drop by spoonfuls on greased cookie sheet. Allow to cool.

pecan pralines

1 C brown sugar
1 C white sugar
½ C light cream
2 TB butter
1 C pecan halves

Dissolve sugars in cream and boil to the thread test, 228 degrees F. stirring occasionally. Add the butter and pecans, cook until syrup reaches 236 degrees F. or forms a soft ball in water. Cool. Beat until somewhat thickened and drop by tablespoon onto a greased marble slab or double thickness of waxed paper. The candy will flatten out into large cakes. Makes 12 pralines.

bourbon balls

Candy is dandy

1 12-oz box vanilla wafers, crumbled
1 C chopped pecans or walnuts
1 C powdered sugar
2 TB sifted cocoa
4 oz bourbon, brandy or Grand Marnier

Mix all ingredients well. Roll into balls, then roll in more powdered sugar or bitter cocoa or melted chocolate. May be stored in plastic bag with additional powdered sugar. May be refrigerated or frozen.

honey graham brittle

½ lb sweet butter
1 C dark brown sugar
1 C chopped pecans
12 honey graham crackers

Bring butter and sugar to a boil. Boil for 2-3 minutes stirring constantly. Remove from heat. Add nuts. Line ungreased 10 x 15 cookie sheet with 12 whole honey grahams. Pour mixture and spread evenly on top. Bake 10 minutes at 350 degrees. Cut while warm. Cool and remove from pan.

chocolate butter crunch

⅛ lb butter
½ C sugar
1/3 C *chopped* nuts, mixed with a pinch of salt
2/3 C *ground* nuts, mixed with a pinch of salt
1 8-oz bar of semi-sweet chocolate

Melt butter in a sauce pan. Add sugar slowly and stir until sugar is incorporated. Allow to settle for a minute, then stir. Continue to do this until the mixture becomes a light brown syrup. Add the *ground* nuts and stir all together. Pour this mixture ⅛" thick onto a greased cookie sheet. Cool. Melt the chocolate. Spread ½ of the chocolate over the candy mixture. Sprinkle ½ of the *chopped* nuts over this. When this all hardens, turn it onto another *ungreased* cookie sheet. Spread the rest of the melted chocolate onto the candy, then sprinkle on the rest of the *chopped* nuts.

english toffee

1½ C softened butter
1½ C sugar
1 tsp light corn syrup
1 C unblanched almonds, split in halves
12 oz semi-sweet chocolate
½ C grated blanched almonds

Melt butter in a heavy saucepan. Add sugar and corn syrup and bring to a boil, stirring constantly with a wooden spoon. The sugar and butter will blend at 250 degrees. Cook over medium heat, stirring constantly, until thermometer registers 290 degrees. Maintain heat at a temperature high enough to keep syrup bubbling. If separation does occur, add 1 TB cold water to mixture and cook until the temperature again reaches 290 degrees.

Remove saucepan from heat and pour the candy onto a large baking pan, tray or marble slab to cool and set. Melt half the chocolate and spread it over the surface of the candy. Sprinkle with half the grated almonds. When the chocolate coating has set, turn candy over and coat the other side with the remaining melted chocolate and grated almonds. Cool and break into pieces.

butterscotch cheese crunchies

6 oz butterscotch morsels
3 TB butter
1 C graham cracker crumbs
1 C finely chopped nuts
½ tsp grated lemon rind
8 oz cream cheese, softened
¼ C sugar
2 TB flour
2 eggs
1 TB lemon juice

Melt butterscotch and butter together over hot water. Remove from heat and stir in crumbs, nuts and lemon rind. Press half of this mixture into 9″ square baking pan. Bake at 350 degrees for 12 minutes.

In mixing bowl, beat cream cheese and sugar until creamy. Add eggs, one at a time, beating well after each addition. Blend in flour and lemon juice. Pour evenly over hot baked crust. Top with other half of crumb mixture. Bake at 350 degrees for 25 minutes.

Cool completely. Cut into 2¼″ x 1″ bars. Refrigerate. Makes 36 bars.

mazeltov mandel bread

1 C sugar
1 C oil
4 eggs
3½ C flour, sifted with 1 TB baking powder
¼ tsp salt
1 C chopped walnuts
rind and juice of 1 lemon

Beat sugar and oil together for 15 minutes. Add the beaten eggs. Add flour, salt, baking powder, walnuts and lemon juice and rind gradually until mixture forms a ball. Divide into 3 15 inch long rolls, adding flour as you roll. Place on ungreased cookie sheet.

Bake at 350 degrees for 20 minutes. Remove from oven. Slice immediately while warm. Lay slices on cookie sheet. Return to 350 degree oven and toast until golden brown.

chocolate hazelnut squares

1 1/3 C hazelnuts, roasted and ground
4 oz plus 1 TB butter
½ C sugar
4 eggs, separated
7 oz semi sweet chocolate, grated
1 TB flour
1-1½ 10oz jar currant jelly
chocolate sprinkles

Preheat oven to 350 degrees. Roast hazelnuts in heavy roasting pan stirring occasionally. Set aside when browned. Remove skin. Grind.

Cream butter, add sugar and egg yolks and beat with mixer until light in color and thick in texture. Add chocolate and hazelnuts. Mix well. Add flour and stir until well blended.

Beat egg whites and fold into mixture. Spread on 2 10 x 15 cookie sheets that have been slightly buttered.

Bake in 350 degree oven for 20 minutes. Do not overbake. Cookies should be soft inside. Remove from oven and spread currant jelly over entire sheet. Sprinkle with chocolate sprinkles.

Cut into 2″ x 2″ squares and remove to rack to cool. When storing in tin or plastic container place wax paper between each row of cookies.

krispie kookies

1 C sugar
1 C light corn syrup
1 C chunky peanut butter
6 C Rice Krispies
12 oz chocolate bits

In a 3 quart sauce pan cook sugar and syrup together until boiling. Stir in peanut butter and Rice Krispies. Press into buttered 10″ x 15″ jelly roll pan. With wet hands press down until smooth. Melt the chocolate in double boiler. Spread over mixture. Chill at least 5 hours. Cut into bars. Keeps and travels very well.

chocolate marshmallow roll

2 squares unsweetened chocolate
1 egg
1 tsp vanilla
2 TB margarine
½ C powdered sugar
2 C miniature marshmallows (multi-color)
12 oz shredded coconut

Melt chocolate in teflon pan (1 or 1½ qt size) over very low flame. Cool for minute. Melt margarine, add egg, vanilla and powdered sugar to chocolate mixture. Stir until dissolved. Add marshmallows and stir until all are coated.

Sprinkle coconut generously on a sheet of wax paper about 18″ long. Drop a mound of 2 or 3 large spoonfuls of coated marshmallows onto wax paper. Roll over coconut by lifting the closest edge of the wax paper and rolling away from you. Then lifting the farthest edges of the wax paper, roll toward you at the same time lightly pressing the marshmallows to form a long roll. Add more coconut generously and roll away from you and toward you as before. Continue this process with the coconut until marshmallows are evenly covered.

Place in refrigerator and chill. Chill and slice. Yield: 30-40 slices. Can be frozen.

golden brownies

½ C butterscotch chips
¼ C butter
¾ C flour
1/3 C brown sugar, packed
1 tsp baking powder
¼ tsp salt
½ tsp vanilla
1 egg
1 C miniature marshmallows
1 C semi-sweet chocolate chips
¼ C chopped nuts

Melt butterscotch chips and butter in a large heavy saucepan over medium heat, stirring constantly. Cool to lukewarm. Add flour, brown sugar, baking powder, salt, vanilla and egg. Mix well. Fold marshmallows, chocolate chips and chopped nuts into batter mixture until just combined, about 5 strokes.

Spread in greased 9″ square pan. Bake in 350 degree oven for 20 to 25 minutes. Do not overbake; the center will be soft, but will become firm upon cooling. Cut into bars.

chocolate nuggets

No cooking, just mix and shape!

6 oz semi-sweet chocolate pieces
3 TB corn syrup
1 tsp vanilla
½ C evaporated milk
½ C powdered sugar
2½ C vanilla wafer crumbs (8 oz)
1 C nuts, finely ground

NUGGET COATING
1½ C finely cut nuts or chocolate sprinkles

Stir chocolate pieces in a 2 quart bowl over hot (not boiling) water until melted. Remove from water. Stir in corn syrup, and vanilla. Gradually stir in evaporated milk, sugar, wafer crumbs and nuts. Mix well. Let stand about 30 minutes. Shape into 1″ balls and roll in about ¾ C chocolate sprinkles or finely chopped nuts. Chill. Makes 4½ dozen.

hamentashen with nuts and honey

NUT-HONEY FILLING (do ahead)
2 C honey
2½ C chopped nuts, walnuts or pecans
1 lemon, juice and grated rind
1 tsp cinnamon

Heat honey at low to medium heat in a large pan. Add nuts, lemon juice and cinnamon. Cook slowly until candy mixture is thick, about 45-60 minutes. When cool enough to handle, shape into triangles, using approximately one TB of the nut mixture. Set on large platter. Triangles will be hard as nut mixture cools.

COOKIE DOUGH
2/3 C sugar
½ lb butter minus 2 TB
2 TB solid shortening
3 eggs
1 tsp vanilla
grated rind of 1 orange
4 C flour (white or whole wheat pastry flour)
2 tsp baking powder
1 TB orange juice, more if needed

Cream sugar, butter and shortening. Add eggs one at a time. Add vanilla and orange rind. Sift flour with baking powder and stir into egg mixture. Add orange juice if necessary to moisten dough. Mix and knead lightly into a roll. Refrigerate for an hour. Toss on slightly floured board, roll out to ⅛″ thickness and cut circles 3-3½″ across. Place triangle nut filling in the center of each round. Moisten outer edge of circle with wet finger; then draw up the three sides and pinch together to form a triangle. Place on a cookie sheet, covered with foil, then greased and floured. Bake at 350 degrees for 25-30 minutes until nicely browned.

This is a Roumanian recipe. It takes a bit of doing but it is worth it — to other Roumanians.

wheat germ cookie puffs

1½ C flour
¾ C wheat germ, regular or sugar and honey
⅛ tsp salt
1 C softened butter or margarine
1/3 C sugar
1 tsp vanilla
1 tsp grated lemon rind
powdered sugar

Combine flour, wheat germ and salt on wax paper. Cream butter, sugar, vanilla and lemon rind thoroughly. Add blended dry ingredients to creamed mixture. Mix well. Press with fingers until it holds together. Shape into 1 inch balls.

Place on ungreased cookie sheet. Bake 350 degrees for 12 to 15 minutes. Sprinkle powdered sugar on cookies while slightly warm. Store in loosely covered container. Makes 30-36 cookies.

chocolate chippies

1¾ C graham cracker crumbs
1 large can sweetened condensed milk
¼ lb butter
12 oz chocolate chips

Mix all the ingredients together by hand, putting chips in last to prevent melting. Spread into a greased 9 x 13 pan. Bake in 350 degree oven for 25 minutes. Cool thoroughly before cutting into squares or bars. May be frozen.

peanut butter confection

1 C peanut butter
¾ C honey
1½ C non-fat dry milk powder
½ C bran
½ C peanuts, chopped
1 oz semi-sweet chocolate
1 tsp butter or margarine

Blend peanut butter, honey and dry milk powder until smooth. Stir in peanuts and bran. Spread in a 8" square pan. Melt chocolate with butter and spread over cookie mixture. Refrigerate. Cut in squares.

oatmeal nut cookies

1 C butter
½ C sugar
½ C brown sugar
1 egg
1 tsp vanilla
1½ C flour
1 tsp soda
1 tsp cinnamon
1½ C oatmeal
1 C nuts, finely chopped
½ C white raisins
6 oz chocolate chips, optional

Cream butter and sugars. Add egg and vanilla and beat well. Sift together flour, soda and cinnamon. Add to beaten mixture. Add oatmeal, chopped nuts, raisins and chocolate chips. Roll into balls or drop by teaspoon. Press down and bake on cookie sheet in 350 degree oven for 6 minutes. Cool on cake rack. Keep in covered cookie jar. Makes 6 dozen.

oatmeal lace cookies

1 C sugar
¼ C cream, half and half
½ C light corn syrup
6 oz melted butter
1¼ C oats, uncooked
1 C flour
1 tsp baking powder
1 tsp vanilla

Mix all the above ingredients. Drop by spoonful on greased cookie sheet. Leave space in between. Bake at 375 degrees for 8 minutes. Cool slightly before removing from pan.

They can be molded around a dowel or broom handle while still warm and soft, but they will crisp up very quickly. Delicious as is, or spread one side with melted bittersweet chocolate. These cookies will keep well in a tightly covered cookie jar. 60-80 cookies.

pecan butter fingers

½ lb butter or margarine
½ C powdered sugar
2 C all purpose flour
½ tsp salt (omit if using salted butter)
1 tsp vanilla
1 C finely chopped lightly toasted pecans
powdered sugar for sprinkling

Beat butter and sugar together until creamy and fluffy. Gradually mix in flour. Stir in salt, vanilla and pecans. Using level tablespoons of dough, shape into 2 inch long fingers.

Place on ungreased baking sheets. Bake 15 to 20 minutes at 350 degrees until slightly browned. Sprinkle with sifted powder sugar. Remove from baking sheets and cool completely. Makes 48 cookies.

wholewheat chocolate chip mandelbread

½ lb butter or margarine
1 1/3 C sugar
6 eggs
2 tsp vanilla
4 C wholewheat pastry flour
2 tsp cinnamon
2 tsp baking powder
1 C chopped nuts
1 1/3 C mini chocolate chips

Cream margarine and sugar. Add eggs and vanilla. Sift together flour, cinnamon and baking powder. Add to egg-sugar mixture. Mix well. Add nuts and chocolate chips. Divide into four portions and form long narrow loaves or rolls. Place on greased cookie sheet. Bake at 350 degrees for about 20 minutes.

Cut loaves diagonally into ¾″ slices and lay pieces on cut side. Bake another 20 minutes or until nicely browned. Makes 5 to 6 dozen cookies.

sesame seed cookies

Sesame bessame

2½ C sesame seed, toasted
6 heaping TB flour
6 heaping TB sugar
6 TB oil
2 eggs
1 tsp vanilla

Mix sesame seeds, flour, sugar and oil together in a bowl. Add the eggs and vanilla. Leave overnight in refrigerator. Shape into small crescents. Bake on greased pan for 20 minutes in a 350 degree oven. Turn off oven and let stand in oven for 15 minutes. Take out and store in tightly lidded can.

melting moments

½ lb butter (or ½ butter and ½ margarine)
1/3 C powdered sugar
¾ C cornstarch
1 C flour
1 tsp vanilla

Mix well all the above ingredients and chill for one hour. Form into balls, press down slightly and bake until golden brown. Bake at 350 degrees for 15 to 20 minutes.

snowballs

1 C butter or margarine
½ C sugar
1½ C plus 2 TB flour
1 tsp vanilla
3 oz cream cheese
½ C chopped nuts, optional
powdered sugar

Mix well then chill. Roll into 2 inch balls. Bake 15 minutes at 375 degrees. While warm roll in a bowl of powdered sugar and let sit to dry.

miniature meltaways

¼ lb butter
1 oz unsweetened chocolate
¼ C granulated sugar
1 tsp vanilla
1 egg beaten
2 C graham cracker crumbs
1 C coconut, shredded
½ C chopped nuts

4 TB butter or margarine
1 TB milk or cream or mocha mix
2 C confectioners sugar, sifted
1 tsp vanilla
2½ oz unsweetened chocolate

Melt butter and chocolate in small pan. Blend sugar, vanilla, egg, crumbs, coconut and nuts into butter-chocolate mixture. Mix well and press into ungreased baking dish 11 x 7. Refrigerate.

Mix butter, milk, confectioners sugar and 1 tsp vanilla. Spread over crumb mixture. Chill in refrigerator. Melt unsweetened chocolate and spread evenly over chilled filling. Immediately cut into 1" squares or even smaller and remove from pan. Makes 3-4 dozen confections. May be frozen.

toffee cookies

½ lb butter or margarine
1 C brown sugar, firmly packed
1 egg yolk
1 tsp vanilla
2 C flour
12 oz chocolate bits
8 oz chopped nuts, optional

Cream sugar and butter. Add egg yolk and vanilla. Mix well, add flour and beat until smooth. Pour into ungreased 10" x 15" cookie sheet. Bake in a 350 degree oven for 20 to 25 minutes. Melt chocolate over boiling water. Spread over cookies while still warm — not hot. Cut cookies into squares. If desired sprinkle with crushed nuts.

banana daiquiri souffle

1 pkg unflavored gelatin
⅛ tsp salt
¼ C sugar
2 eggs, separated, plus 1 egg white
¾ C water
2½ large ripe bananas
¼ C lime juice, (2 limes)
¼ C light rum
½ C frozen whipped topping, thawed, or whipped cream
pinch of cream of tartar
toasted nuts

In heavy saucepan stir gelatin, salt and half of sugar. On low heat gradually stir in egg yolks, one at a time, and the water. Cook over low heat, stirring frequently, until gelatin is completely dissolved, about 5 minutes. Mixture should not boil. Remove from heat.

Slice bananas into blender. Add lime juice and rum. Blend until well-mixed. Stir banana mixture into gelatin mixture until well blended. Refrigerate until mixture mounds slightly when dropped from spoon, about one hour or less.

Meantime, make collar for 1 qt souffle dish. Pour banana mixture into large bowl, and add beaten cream. Beat egg whites, gradually adding remaining sugar and pinch of cream of tartar. Beat stiff. With wire whisk gently combine. Pour into souffle dish. Refrigerate overnight. When ready to serve, garnish with slices of bananas and toasted nuts.

blueberry betty

1 qt fresh blueberries or 2 10-oz pkg frozen
1 TB lemon juice
¼ tsp cinnamon
1 C flour
1 C sugar
½ C butter

Place berries in 1½ qt casserole. Add lemon juice, sprinkle cinnamon. In a separate bowl sift together flour and sugar and chop butter into mixture. Spread over berries. Bake in 375 degree oven for 45 minutes. Serve with ice cream or whipped cream.

blender chocolate mousse

6 oz semi-sweet chocolate
2 TB coffee liqueur
3 TB orange juice
2 egg yolks
2 whole eggs
1 tsp vanilla extract
¼ C sugar
1 C heavy cream

Melt chocolate in the liqueur and juice over low heat and set aside to cool. Put the eggs, yolks, sugar and vanilla in the blender — mix for 2 minutes at medium speed. Add cream and blend for 30 seconds more. Add the melted and cooled chocolate and blend till smooth. Pour into 6 small custard cups or porcelain "pots-de-creme" and chill for several hours. May be topped with whipped cream.

chocolate mousse
You won't miss the whipping cream

4 oz semi-sweet chocolate
¼ C strong coffee
1 TB Cognac
5 eggs, separated

Melt chocolate and coffee in double boiler over very hot but not boiling water. Remove double boiler from heat but leave mixture over hot water. Separate eggs. Add egg yolks to chocolate mixture one at a time carefully. Cool mixture. Add Cognac.

Beat egg whites until stiff. Fold gently into chocolate mixture. Pour mixture into 1 qt souffle dish, or individual glasses. Chill. Tastes even better made a day ahead and refrigerated. May be decorated with slivered or whole blanched almonds.

ice cream charlotte
*As Scarlett O'Hara might say: "fiddle dee dee
I'll think about those calories tomorrow"*

1 pkg ladyfingers
1 qt chocolate ice cream
1 qt vanilla ice cream
1 qt coffee ice cream (or any combination you like)
1 lb English toffee candy crushed
Chocolate Fudge Sauce

Place lady fingers around sides of one 9″-10″ spring form pan. Layer ice cream and candy twice. Start with ice cream and end with crushed toffee on top. Serve with heated fudge sauce.

chocolate fudge sauce

1 oz unsweetened chocolate
1 6 oz package semi-sweet chocolate chips
½ C white Karo syrup
1 tsp instant coffee dissolved in 1 TB hot water
1 tsp vanilla or cream de cocoa or rum
½ C sour cream

Melt chocolate over hot water. Remove from flame. Stir in syrup, then add the rest of the ingredients, stirring in sour cream last a little at a time. Makes 1 pt. Refrigerate in covered jar.

pareve ice cream

This comes from South Africa where it is very popular at Bar Mitzvahs

1 10-oz carton non-dairy whipping cream
3 eggs separated
1/3 C sugar
6 oz Halvah

Whip cream. Beat yolks with sugar until thick and creamy. Fold in whipped cream. Beat egg whites until stiff and fold into cream mixture. Flake Halvah with a fork or in processor. Mix it all together and freeze.

cream puffs

1 C water
½ C solid shortening
¼ tsp salt
1 C sifted flour
4 eggs, at room temperature

Bring water, shortening and salt to a boil. Stir in flour all at once and cook until dough forms a smooth ball and leaves sides of saucepan clean. Remove from heat and cool slightly. Add eggs, one at a time, beating well after each addition. Drop by spoonfuls on a greased cookie sheet. Bake at 450 degrees for 10 minutes. Reduce heat to 400 degrees and bake 25 minutes longer. Cool, slit and fill. Makes 12 very large puffs. To make 48 miniatures, bake at 400 degrees, 25 minutes.

VANILLA CUSTARD FILLING
5 TB flour
½ C sugar
¼ tsp salt
2 C liquid non-dairy cream
2 egg yolks, unbeaten
1 TB margarine
1 tsp vanilla

Mix flour, sugar and salt together in sauce pan. Add small amount of cream and mix to form a smooth paste. Add egg yolks and beat thoroughly. Add remaining creamer and blend. Place over medium heat and cook 5-7 minutes, stirring constantly until smooth and thick. Add margarine, cool. Add vanilla. Fill 12 large puffs. Top with melted chocolate sauce. Refrigerate.

top hat baked apples

4 roman beauty apples
24 red hot cinnamon pieces
8 walnut pieces
4 tsp brown sugar
8 marshmallows

Core apples. Trim down one inch. Fill centers with 5 red hots and 2 walnut pieces per apple. Sprinkle with brown sugar. Place in baking dish which has 1 inch of water. Add a few more red hots and walnut pieces. Cover with foil. Bake 40-45 minutes at 375 degrees. Baste. Remove cover. Baste again. Bake a few more minutes until soft. Cool a few minutes. Top each with 2 marshmallows and another red hot. Baste again. Should be rosy and beautiful.

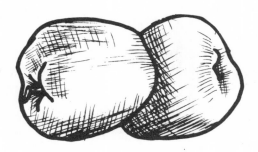

english trifle

Line your prettiest deep glass bowl or serving dish with slices of sponge cake or with sandwiches made of sponge cake and strawberry jam. Pour sweet red wine, sherry or rum over the cake. Cover with any red jello made according to directions on box. After jello begins to set, add canned fruit like peaches, pears, pineapple or any fruit you have on hand. Or use fresh fruit like bananas, pineapple chunks, grapes or frozen drained raspberries.

Make custard* with vanilla pudding or chocolate custard pudding and cover the fruit in the bowl. Allow to set. Cover with ½ pt sweetened whipped cream and decorate with candied cherries or strawberries and sliced roasted almonds around the edge. Make the day before serving. It tastes even better.

*Try this processor custard recipe

1 C milk
1 C sour cream
1 pkg instant vanilla pudding

Mix together and process for 5 seconds. Scrape sides and process 5 seconds longer. Do not over process.

caramel custard

¾ C sugar for caramel sauce
1 qt milk
8 eggs
½ C sugar
¼ tsp salt
1½ tsp vanilla
pinch nutmeg

To caramelize ¾ cup sugar, use a shallow small frying pan and stir the sugar until it becomes liquid. Keep stirring at moderate heat and watch carefully as mixture begins to turn a light brown color. Do not overcook as it will taste bitter. Pour into baking dish or mold and tilt so caramel will spread around. Heat milk until just below boiling. Beat eggs and sugar in large bowl until well mixed. Add salt. Pour hot milk into egg mixture and continue beating with wire whisk. Add vanilla and strain through a fine sieve into the baking dish. Sprinkle nutmeg lightly on top of custard.

Place shallow pan of water into a 325 degree oven. Set the baking dish into the water and bake for about 45 minutes or until knife inserted in the middle of custard comes out clean and custard is set. Remove from water bath. Chill or serve hot if desired. Unmold by inverting mold on serving dish when ready to serve. Dish should be deep enough for the caramel sauce, which will be melted.

chocolate dipped strawberries
Fantastic finale for special occasions

Wash and dry about 30 long stemmed giant strawberries. Melt 8 ounces good quality bitter-sweet chocolate over simmering water in a double boiler. Add 1 TB oil, blend well. Dip the tip of each strawberry into the chocolate. Set in a broiler pan rack, stem side down. Chill in the refrigerator.

chocolate leaves

Thoroughly wash and dry 12 camellia leaves. Melt 2 ounces good quality bitter-sweet chocolate over simmering water in a double boiler. Using the back of a spoon, spread the underside of the leaves thickly with chocolate, keeping the edges clean. Place on a cookie tray chocolate side up and put in the freezer. When frozen, carefully peel leaf from chocolate leaf. May be stored in a covered container in the freezer for several weeks. Use to decorate ice cream, mousse or cakes.

strawberry mousse dessert

Our national president loved it when she visited Beverly Hills

3 oz strawberry, raspberry or cherry jello
1 pt frozen berries
½ pt whipping cream, (non-dairy cream may be used)
more whipped cream for garnish

Defrost berries. Make jello following directions on the box, using juice of the berries. When jello begins to jell add berries and whipped cream. Pour into 6-8 champagne glasses. Chill.

For a lovely charlotte, double the recipe. Line a 9" spring form pan with ladyfingers. Pour in the mousse. Garnish with additional whipped cream and berries.

In raspberry season, add some fresh whole raspberries to mixture, or in the bottom of individual glasses.

frozen macaroon mousse

A centerpiece that makes your table a Valentine

¾ C sugar
1/3 C water
3 egg yolks
dash salt
1 C crumbled almond macaroons (10)
4 lady fingers, split
2 TB Grand Marnier
1½ C chilled heavy cream
2 tsp vanilla
½ tsp almond extract

RASPBERRY SAUCE
2 pkg frozen raspberries, thawed
2 TB cornstarch
½ C currant jelly

TOPPING
4 oz milk chocolate
½ C chilled heavy cream

In small pan mix sugar with 1/3 C water. Bring to a boil over medium heat, stirring to dissolve sugar. Boil gently, but do not stir, to 230 degrees F. on candy thermometer or until a little spins a thread when dropped from a spoon. In another medium bowl, with mixer at medium speed, beat egg yolks and salt until light. Gradually beat in hot syrup in thin stream. Continue beating until mixture begins to cool, about 2 minutes. Add macaroons. Refrigerate ½ hour. Sprinkle lady fingers with Grand Marnier. Beat cream with vanilla and almond extracts until stiff. Fold whipped cream into macaroon mixture. Line 6 to 7 C mold* with foil. Turn ½ of mixture into mold. Cover with ladyfingers. Pour rest of mixture on top. Freeze until firm, for about 4 hours.

To make raspberry sauce, drain berries, reserving the liquid. Add water to make 2 C. In small saucepan blend liquid with cornstarch. Boil 5 minutes over medium heat, stirring constantly. Stir in jelly until dissolved. Remove from heat. Add raspberries. Refrigerate covered.

To make chocolate curls, place wrapped chocolate bar in warm place to soften, but not melt. With a vegetable peeler pressing lightly, pare along bar in long thin strokes to form curls.

To assemble: Beat ½ C cream until stiff. Unmold frozen mold onto chilled shallow serving dish. Spoon raspberry sauce around base. Decorate with whipped cream, using No. 5 decorating tip. Garnish with chocolate curls. Serves 10 to 12.

*Its worth investing in a heart-shaped mold.

papaya supreme

We all loved it at the dinner dance and asked for more

2 medium papayas
32 strawberries — fresh or frozen
4 egg whites
8 TB sugar

Cut papayas in half. Remove seeds. Place 8 strawberries in each half. Beat egg whites until frothy. Add sugar gradually until whites stand in stiff peaks. Cover papayas with egg white topping, sealing edges neatly. Place in a broiler pan and broil until whites become golden brown (approximately 30 seconds). Place each half on a plate with a paper doily. Serves 4.

frozen lemon cream

Featherlight

1½ C vanilla wafer or graham cracker crumbs
1½ C sugar
¾ C lemon juice (3-4 lemons)
6 eggs, separated
¼ tsp salt
3 C heavy cream, whipped

Line the bottom of a 9″ spring form pan with 1 C of crumbs. Dissolve sugar in lemon juice. Set aside. In a large mixing bowl, beat egg yolks with salt. Add the lemon mixture. Beat 3-4 minutes until thick and creamy. Fold in the whipped cream. Beat egg whites until stiff. Fold into mixture. Pour into form. Top with remaining crumbs (optional). Wrap with foil and freeze. When ready to serve, unmold and place on serving platter, in refrigerator 2½-3 hours before serving.

206

strawberry "sorbet"

A refreshing, delicious, low-calorie treat

2 baskets fresh strawberries
        or
1 lb pkg frozen, unsweetned strawberries
1 ripe banana
1 TB sugar, or sugar substitute
1 TB Grand Marnier (optional)

Puree the berries, banana, sugar and liqueur in a blender or processor until the sorbet is smooth. Freeze for a few hours. Thaw for about 1 hour before serving. Serve in pretty crystal dishes or grapefruit, orange or melon shells. Serves 6.

Try raspberries, peaches or very ripe pineapple.

Sing a song of sixpence
Bake yourself a pie.
Make it tangy, tart or sweet.
The compliments will fly.

For easier handling, roll out all pie crust dough between two sheets of wax paper.

pie crusts
You've got a lot of crust here

FOOD PROCESSOR METHOD
1. Use steel blade.
2. Use frozen or very cold sweet butter, margarine or solid vegetable shortening.
3. Use bleached, pre-sifted all purpose flour, or instant flour.
4. To prevent soggy crust, brush slightly beaten egg white over crust before adding filling.
5. One recipe for 9″ crust also makes 8 3″ tarts.
6. Let dough "sit" and chill 30 minutes to make rolling easier.

TO PROCESS
Cut the shortening and butter in pieces. Place in work bowl. Add flour. Process carefully until mixture resembles coarse meal. Add liquid (chilled) a few drops at a time through tube while machine is going, until it starts to vibrate and dough starts to form a ball. Let dough "sit" and chill. Roll dough out between two sheets of wax paper. Place in lightly greased pie pan. Prick sides and bottom. Cover with buttered foil, buttered side touching dough. Weigh down with rice (which can be stored and reused). Bake 10 minutes in preheated 425 degree oven. Remove foil and rice, and bake another 10 minutes. If edges get too dark, cover with strips of foil.

9″ FLAKY CRUST
1 1/3 C to 1½ C flour
¼ lb butter or a combination of
    4 TB butter and 4 TB shortening
⅛-¼ C ice cold water
¼ tsp salt

10″ RICH PIE CRUST
1½ C flour
2 TB solid vegetable shortening
4 TB butter
⅛ tsp salt
¼ C cream, half and half

chocolate graham cracker crumb crust

3 TB butter or margarine
3 TB shortening
¾ C graham cracker crumbs (15 graham crackers)
¾ C instant cocoa mix (or 3 1-oz pkgs)
3 TB sugar (optional)

Melt butter and shortening together. Combine cocoa mix, graham cracker crumbs and sugar and blend in shortening. Press firmly into 9″ pie pan. Bake at 350 degrees for 8 minutes. Cool before filling.

NUTTY CHOCOLATE CRUMB CRUST
¾ C crushed chocolate wafers
1/3 C finely chopped walnuts
4 TB sugar
4 TB melted butter

Press into 9″ pie plate.
Refrigerate at least 4 hours.

chocolate coconut pie shell

2 oz unsweetened chocolate
2 TB butter
2 TB hot milk
2/3 C powdered sugar
1½ C finely chopped coconut
½ C finely chopped nuts (optional)

Melt chocolate and butter together over hot water. Mix milk and sugar. Add to chocolate mixture. Stir well. Add coconut and chopped nuts. Spread evenly into an 8″ pie pan. Fill with ice cream and freeze.

pie crust medley

NUTTY CRUMB CRUST
¾ C graham cracker crumbs
1/3 C finely chopped almonds,
    walnuts or pecans
2 TB brown sugar
3 TB melted butter or margarine

Press into 9" pie plate.
Bake in 350 degrees 8 minutes.

WAFER CRUST
¾ C crushed vanilla wafers
1/3 C finely chopped walnuts
4 TB brown sugar
4 TB melted butter

Press into 9" pie plate.
Refrigerate at least 4 hours.

BUTTER CRUST
1½ C graham cracker crumbs
4 TB ground walnuts
2 TB sugar
1 tsp grated lemon peel
6 TB melted butter

Bake in 350 degrees 8 minutes.

SESAME CRUST
4 TB sesame seeds
1 C sifted flour
½ tsp salt
1/3 C butter or margarine
3-4 TB cold water

Toast sesame seeds in 325 degrees for 8-10 minutes. Mix seeds with flour and salt in a bowl. Cut in butter until mixture has texture of small peas. Sprinkle water into mixture a little at a time while tossing and stirring lightly with a fork. Roll out on a floured board to a circle 1½" larger than a 9" pie pan. Fit loosely into pan. Flute rim. Prick with a fork. Bake at 400 degrees for 10-12 minutes. Excellent with quiche filling.

9″ SWEET PIE CRUST (Sucree or Meurbe)
1½ C flour
¼ lb butter
1½ TB sugar
½ tsp baking powder
¼ tsp plain vinegar
1-2 tsp ice water

fruit pie or flan

1 baked 9″ cookie crust*

Wash and hull fresh blueberries, strawberries, raspberries, boysenberries or sliced peaches. Dry thoroughly. Arrange artistically on the crust.

SYRUP FOR GLAZE

Melt a 10 oz jar of strawberry or apple jelly in a suacepan over low heat. Cool. Spoon over the fruit. Or make your own glaze by combining the following:

¼ C sugar
1 C water
2 tsp cornstarch
2 TB jam or jelly

Simmer sugar, water and cornstarch together until thickened. Add any flavor strained jam or jelly. When thick, clear and cool, spoon over the fruit.

*The crust may be made a day ahead, but the tart tastes better if the fruit and glaze are assembled the same day as they are served.

WALNUT CRUST
1¼ C finely chopped walnuts
3 TB sugar
2 TB butter or margarine, melted
¼ C flour

Combine ingredients in a 9″ pie pan. Press mixture evenly against bottom and sides of pan. Bake at 400 degrees for 10 minutes. Cool completely before filling.

black bottom pie

1 9″ baked pie shell

BASIC CREAM
16 oz milk
½ C sugar
3 eggs, separated
5 TB cornstarch
¼ tsp salt
1 TB gelatin
¼ C water
1½ oz chocolate, unsweetened
½ tsp vanilla
1 TB rum
½ pt whipping cream
2 TB sugar
1 oz chocolate bar, semi-sweet for chocolate swirls

Cook milk, sugar, egg yolks, cornstarch, and salt in a double boiler until thick like pudding. Sprinkle gelatin over water. When dissolved mix into basic cream mixture. Cool. Divide into 2 bowls equally. Melt chocolate and mix into one bowl of basic cream. Add vanilla. Beat egg whites until stiff. Fold into the other bowl of basic cream. Add rum.

When both mixtures are cool and begin to thicken, pour chocolate part into the pie shell and cover with the basic cream mixture. Whip cream, add sugar and put a thin layer over top of pie. Make chocolate curls with a potato peeler and arrange on top. Refrigerate until time to serve.

apricot coconut pie

CRUST
**6 oz coconut flakes pressed into a greased 9" pie
plate**

Bake in 325 degree oven 10 to 15 minutes until golden brown. Cool.

FILLING
**1 envelope gelatin
1/3 tsp sugar
12 oz apricot nectar
1 tsp lemon juice
1 tsp almond extract or Amaretto liqueur
2 unbeaten egg whites**

Heat nectar and pour over gelatin and sugar to dissolve. Add lemon juice and almond extract. Chill until syrup thickens slightly. Add unbeaten egg whites. Beat with electric beater for 10 minutes. Pour into coconut shell and chill. Top with whipping cream. Sliced apricots may be added for decoration.

almond toffee pie

**½ C milk
3 eggs, separated
2 tsp vanilla
½ C brown sugar, packed
½ pint whipping cream
1 C ground almond toffee
1 10" graham cracker or chocolate graham
cracker pie shell**

Combine milk, egg yolks, 1 tsp vanilla and sugar in top of double boiler. Cook over boiling water until mixture coats a spoon. Cool thoroughly in refrigerator about 30 minutes stirring often.

Beat egg whites until stiff. Whip cream. Fold together egg whites, whipped cream and remaining vanilla. Add ½ C ground toffee to egg yolk mixture. Fold all into egg white and cream mixture. Pour filling into crust. Top with remaining ground toffee and freeze. Serve frozen. Serves 10-12.

blueberry cheesecake pie

CRUST
7 oz vanilla wafers, crushed
½ C walnuts, chopped (2¾ oz)
6 TB brown sugar
6 TB melted butter

Combine wafers, walnuts, sugar and butter. Press into a 10″-11″ spring form or large pie plate. Refrigerate overnight.

FILLING
8 oz cream cheese at room temperature
1 C powdered sugar
1 tsp vanilla
1 pint whipping cream

Cream together cheese, sugar and vanilla. Whip cream until stiff and fold into cheese mixture. Spread into chilled shell.

TOPPING
1 can (21 oz) blueberry pie filling
1 tsp lemon juice

Stir lemon juice into blueberry pie filling. Spoon carefully all over cake. Chill 6-8 hours. Serves 14.

lemon yogurt pie

CRUST
1 C walnuts, chopped
1 C graham crackers, crushed
3 TB sugar
3 TB butter, melted

Combine all ingredients and pat into 9" pie pan. Bake crust for 15 minutes at 350 degrees. Cool.

FILLING
2 8 oz containers lemon yogurt
1 medium size frozen whipped topping
rind of 1 lemon
3 TB lemon juice

Mix and blend the yogurt with the lemon and topping. Pour mixture into cooled crust; chill in refrigerator until set.

BLUEBERRY YOGURT PIE VARIATION
2 8oz containers blueberry yogurt
1 medium size frozen whipped topping
2 15oz cans blueberries, drained

Mix yogurt with whipped topping. Add 1 can blueberries. Place mixture in graham cracker crust. Top with remaining blueberries. Refrigerate. Make early in the morning or the day before.

deep dish sherry apple charlotte

Hush hush sweet Charlotte

Double your favorite sweet pie crust recipe. Use 9" x 3" spring form pan.

FILLING
4 TB flour
½ C brown sugar
⅛ tsp salt
6 C apples (about 8 apples) tart, firm,
     peeled cut in chunks
1½ tsp lemon juice
½ tsp nutmeg
1 tsp cinnamon
1 TB grated lemon peel
¼ C dry sherry
1½ C raisins and currants
½ C chopped nuts
1 egg yolk
1 TB milk

Line bottom and sides of pan with 2/3 of the pie crust mixture. Brush with slightly beaten egg white. Place in freezer for about 1 hour. Spread ¼ C corn flake crumbs over frozen bottom of crust.

Mix filling ingredients together. Place filling into pan. Dot with a little butter. Place top crust on and seal edges. Flute rim. Brush top with egg yolk combined with a little milk. Prick crust to let steam escape. Bake on lower shelf at 425 degrees for 45 minutes. Sprinkle with sugar.

Can also be frozen before baking. On serving day, prick crust. Bake on lower shelf at 500 degrees for 15 minutes. Reduce heat to 450 degrees and bake until browned. Sprinkle with sugar and serve at room temperature.

german apple pie

CRUST
1 C all purpose flour
6 TB butter, cut in pieces
2 TB sugar
1 egg yolk
1 TB cold water
⅛ tsp salt

Mix above ingredients on floured board and quickly knead. (If food processor is used, butter must be frozen and cut in pieces. Process with metal blade until ball forms). Roll out and press into 9″ pie pan or spring form.

FILLING
2-3 lb tart, green apples, peeled, quartered and cored
2 TB sugar, if desired

Preheat oven at 375 degrees. Slash apples with sharp knife a few times on the rounded side. Stand apple slices up against side of pie pan going around in a circle. Continue placing apples around with slashed, rounded part toward outside of circle, until pie pan has been filled. There should not be any dough showing when you are through. Fill in bare spots with apple pieces.

Sprinkle sugar over apples, if you desire. Bake until half done, about 30 minutes. Remove from oven and pour topping over apples. Return to oven and finish baking, another 30 minutes, or until topping and crust are well browned.

TOPPING
8 oz sour cream
3 egg yolks
1½ TB sugar
½ tsp vanilla
juice of ½ lemon

Mix above ingredients well and pour over apples.

strawberry cheese pie

1 baked graham cracker pie crust, 9"
8 oz cream cheese
1/3 C sugar
½ C sour cream
1 tsp vanilla
4 oz frozen whipped topping
2 baskets strawberries, reserving one for top
1 C water
2 TB cornstarch
½ C sugar

Beat softened cream cheese, add sugar, sour cream, vanilla and topping. Spoon into crust. Chill at least 2 hours. Wash and hull the strawberries. Crush, and add water. Cook for 5 minutes. Cool and sieve. Mix cornstarch with sugar. Stir into berry mixture. Bring to a boil, stirring constantly. Stir and cook until thick and clear. Cool to room temperature.

Place remaining berries on top. Pour glaze over all. Chill again, at least 2 hours before serving.

pumpkin pie

Crust for 1 10" pie
4 TB butter
1¾ C milk
3½ C pumpkin, mashed
4 eggs, beaten
1 1/3 C sugar
1 tsp salt
1 TB cinnamon
1 tsp nutmeg
½ tsp ground ginger

Melt the butter into hot milk. Mix pumpkin, eggs, sugar, salt, cinnamon, nutmeg and ginger together. Pour into pie shell. Bake at 450 degrees for 15 minutes. Reduce heat to 350 degrees and bake for 30 minutes longer or until filling is set.

hawaiian miracle coconut pie

From Tonde Leyo's kitchen, aka Tante Leia

4 eggs
2 oz butter, melted
1 tsp vanilla
1 C shredded coconut
2 C milk
½ C sugar
½ C flour
¾ tsp baking powder
⅛ tsp salt

Grease 9½" pyrex pie plate. Blend all ingredients in blender for a short time. Pour into pie plate. Bake in preheated 350 degree oven for 40-45 minutes on a cookie sheet — it spills over.

lemon chiffon pie

your favorite 9" pie crust
1 TB granulated gelatin
¼ C cold water
4 eggs, separated
1 C granulated sugar
½ C lemon juice
½ tsp salt
1 tsp grated lemon rind
½ C heavy cream whipped

Bake pie shell in very hot oven (450 degrees) 15-18 minutes. Cool. Soak gelatin in cold water for 5 minutes. Add ½ C sugar, lemon juice and salt to beaten egg yolks and cook on top of double boiler until thick. Add softened gelatin to hot egg custard, and stir until dissolved. Add grated lemon rind. Cool.

Beat egg whites stiff but not dry. Beat remaining ½ C sugar into egg whites. Fold egg whites into cooled egg custard. Pour into cooled baked pie shell. Chill in refrigerator until set. Garnish with whipped cream.

macadamia nut pie

Aloha and shalom

1 9 or 10 inch baked pie crust
2 C milk
½ C sugar
3 egg yolks
¼ tsp salt
5 TB cornstarch
1 TB gelatin
¼ C water
1 tsp vanilla
3 egg whites, beaten
6 oz Macadamia nuts, chopped, salt free*
½ pint whipping cream, optional
2 TB sugar, optional

BASIC CREAM: Cook milk, sugar, egg yolks, salt and cornstarch in a double boiler until thick like pudding, about 10-12 minutes. Sprinkle gelatin over water. When dissolved, mix into basic cream. Add vanilla. Chill. Toast nuts in the oven until light brown. Beat egg whites until stiff. Fold into the basic cream mixture. Fold in 4 oz of the nuts. When mixture is cool and begins to thicken, pour into a cool, baked pie crust. Sprinkle remaining nuts on top. If whipping cream is used sprinkle nuts on top of cream. Refrigerate until time to serve.

*If nuts are salted, wash and dry before chopping.

pecan pie

1 9″ unbaked pie crust
1 C dark corn syrup
1 C pecans, chopped coarsely
½ C granulated sugar
3 eggs
1 tsp vanilla
½ tsp salt

Beat eggs slightly, add sugar, syrup and nuts, salt and vanilla. Put into pie shell and bake 30 minutes in 350 degree oven. The pecans will float to the top forming a crust that will brown nicely if baked slowly.

221

fruit pizza pie

When the moon hits your eye
like a big pizza pie thats amore

1 pkg yellow cake mix
¼ C water
2 eggs
¼ C butter or margarine
¼ C brown sugar, packed
½ C chopped nuts
1 envelope dessert topping mix (for pareve use enough
    non-dairy topping to make 1 C whipped)
        or
10 oz canned vanilla pudding
2 baskets strawberries
1 can pineapple spears or rings, well drained
3 doz grapes
1 banana peeled, sliced and dipped in lemon juice
1 C apricot preserves
4 TB water, brandy or 1 C apple jelly

Combine half the cake mix, water, eggs, butter and brown sugar and mix thoroughly. Blend in remaining cake mix. Fold in nuts. Line 2 12" pizza pans with wax paper. Pour half of batter in each pan. Bake at 350 degrees for 15-20 minutes, until toothpick comes out clean. Cool, and remove from pans.

Freeze one pizza or double the amount of fruit to make 2 pizzas. Prepare topping mix as directed on package, or use pudding. Spread on cake. Wash, hull and lightly sugar strawberries. Reserve choicest ones for center. Arrange fruit in circles on pizza.

To make glaze, heat preserves with liquid until melted. Remove from heat. Strain and cool. Brush on fruit and refrigerate until ready to serve.

INDEX

INDEX

INDEX

INDEX

INDEX

Additional copies of this book may be purchased from
THE BEVERLY HILLS CHAPTER OF HADASSAH
292 South La Cienega Blvd.
Beverly Hills, Ca. 90211
(213) 652-5601

The Hadassah University Hospital
Mt. Scopus, Jerusalem